On t

Brighton Beat

Memoirs of an old-time copper

David Rowland

Finsbury Publishing

200450949

Photograph on title page: the author with the Federation Plate (*see page 202*)

By the same author:
Survivors
The Brighton Blitz
The Coastal Blitz
Out of the Blue
Spitfires Over Sussex: the Exploits of 602 Squadron
War in the City, part 1

British Library Cataloguing-in Publication Data.
A catalogue record for this book is available from the British Library.

ISBN 0-9539392-4-3

Published by Finsbury Publishing, 2 Harvest Close, Telscombe Cliffs,
Peacehaven, East Sussex BN10 7JG

Printed by CPI Antony Rowe Limited, Highfield Industrial Estate, Eastbourne,
East Sussex BN23 6QT

This book is dedicated to my very good friend
Arthur Charles Bishop,
also known as Tony and Bish
4.6.1931–23.7.2005

[Photo courtesy of Mrs Pat Bishop]

Author and Author's Notes

The author was born in 1935 and so spent his childhood during the second world war. He lived from 1939 in a small terraced house in Grove Street, in the heart of a Brighton working class community – a fact to which he often refers and of which he is very proud.

He joined Brighton Police in June 1958 and was medically discharged in February 1985, serving in the force for a little over 26 years.

A number of people contributed their experiences to this book, and the author is especially grateful to Peter Burrows, Ian Wilson, Brian Stanford and Dick Clay BEM. He has also drawn from the book *History of Brighton Police 1838–1967* compiled mainly by Inspector Gerald Baines, a policeman he knew quite well.

Thanks and apologies are due to his long-suffering wife Chris, who has had to tolerate the intrusion of cumbersome files and other paperwork in the house for far too long. Thanks, too, to David Arscott of Pomegranate Press for editing the book and preparing it for publication.

There is more of the history of Brighton Police on display at their old police station in the basement of Brighton town hall. This display lasts throughout the summer from May until October, and a small sum from each book sold will be donated to it.

INTRODUCTION

I have wanted to write a factual story about the Brighton Police for a number of years. I wanted to tell the story of what really went on in a once-proud police force staffed by very proud men and women.

In 1949, aged 14 years and attending the old Fawcett School in York Place, I had soon to come to terms with a job when I left school. Like many kids at that time I had no idea what I wanted to do. My father wanted me to join my uncle and become a carpenter. I was no good with my hands in those days, and I am still pretty useless where that type of skill is involved. My father was a patissier and a very good one, too – perhaps I should work with food. Well, in a way I did, but in food retail: I joined Sainsbury's when I was 15.

In 1953 I was called up for National Service, and in an effort to stay with food I became a cook in the RAF. I had some success with this, and having gradually gained promotion I found myself in charge of the officers' mess at RAF Compton Bassett in Wiltshire.

Five years later I joined the Brighton Police. In the early 1960s, prompted by the threat of nuclear war, so-called 'mobile units' were set up. These would help the public if there were a nuclear attack. It was pretty similar to the wartime ARP, where there was a field kitchen group as part of the mobile unit. My background was known by the police authorities, and so once again I donned my 'blue check trousers and tall white hat' and found myself as a cook – but this time as a police cook. This was something I could never have imagined would happen to me, but it was good fun, apart from the serious side of it.

Over the years I have been asked not only 'What was it like to be a policeman in Brighton', but 'What sort of a policeman were you?' This takes a while to ponder.

The first question is pretty easy, in a way. I believe that I spent the best years of my life being a policeman in Brighton, a wonderful job that on many occasions brought absolute fulfilment to me. On many occasions the end product of a job well done was very personal and certainly made you feel good. The second question, however, is a lot harder to answer.

I was privileged to serve with a large number of very brave policemen for whom I have the greatest respect – people like Constables Dick Clay and Pete Rubridge who were awarded the British Empire Medal for disarming a gunman, putting their own lives in danger. Other BEMs were awarded to 'Johnny' Lock and 'Nobby' Clarke, two other brave guys.

Many other officers were not awarded medals but nevertheless had difficult and dangerous jobs with the varied and different units set up within the police service. I am particularly thinking of squads like the Crime Squad, the Burglary Squad and several other 'secret' squads, made up of teams of specially selected officers. I could never have served in those squads, as that was not my 'scene': it took special people to thrive within them.

I would never claim to be the greatest constable that patrolled the Brighton streets, but by the same token I don't believe I was the

worst. In the early days I was a slim, shy guy who didn't like to be pushy and did my very best not to be noticed by our supervisory staff. I suppose I would have to say that I was more like Dixon of Dock Green rather than Jack Regan of the Sweeney. I didn't win any medals, and the only one I did get I refused to be presented with at headquarters. That was a medal for completing (or was it lasting for) 22 years of 'unblemished' service.

The medal was officially for Good Conduct and Long Service, but in my opinion some officers received the medal whether or not they had been of good conduct, which I believe demeaned the presentation of it. Years later I tried hard to have the medal changed to Long Service only, but that route

'Dog collar' uniform worn by Pc Bob Hampton, on duty outside the Downs Hotel, Woodingdean in the late 1950s. Bob was at Arnhem during the war. [Jonathan Hampton]

was too long and difficult, with representations to the Lord Chamberlain's office. I started along this road but gave it up for lack of interest on the part of some of my colleagues.

I suppose I was quite naive for my age (I was 22 years old when I joined), and in the early days I probably needed a bit of a push or even a good kick to get me started. By the early 1970s my shyness had gone and I was quite 'gobby' and loud: it's strange how you can change over a period of time. Mind, I believe that was more about gaining confidence as the years rolled by.

However, what I do feel is that I carried out my duties in a keen and efficient manner and protected those members of the public more vulnerable that most on the beats on which I served, treating them with fairness and respect.

This is not intended to be a dig against those people who police the local area now. I fully appreciate that times change and people with it, but nevertheless it appears that some respect and efficiency has been lost during the intervening years. One of the reasons could be the amount of work now having to be taken on board by fewer officers both male and female, although at a guess I believe it is because of the massive increase in paperwork to satisfy those people in government.

Unless you served in the force in the 1950s as well as the 2000s it is impossible to make an accurate comment on the differences, good or bad. However, my perception is that the force is not as efficient as it was 40 or 50 years ago, possibly for the reasons that I have mentioned

My story deals with the history of the Brighton force and also with stories from those proud officers who served in the Brighton Borough Police Force during the 1950s through to the 1980s, by which time it had lost its identity and been amalgamated into the current Sussex Police Force with its headquarters at Malling House in Lewes.

Another part of the story is written about the different aspects of the force in which I had the pleasure to serve and about the officers I served with. These include several senior officers who commanded my highest respect and others who didn't. The inspectors, sergeants and constables who I was with day in and day out – the sections that were made into very efficient teams – became like second families.

This story is also about the valuable back-up teams of men and women who at times were the unsung heroes in major investigations into the most serious of crimes.

The book isn't about juicy murders, rapes and other serious offences, but about the mundane things that make up the biggest part of a policeman's life. It is, in part, about the boredom, the soakings in the rain and the lonely night patrols that were undertaken by officers during this period. It is about the unfriendliness of some officers to the new recruits as they tried to get through their probationary period of two years: the period of the recently joined recruits at the training school, which in those days was at Sandgate near Folkestone, was a full thirteen weeks.

These weeks were similar to the initial and trade training I had experienced in the RAF – the square-bashing and the gym work, which I totally disliked. I think the difference was the lack of bullying in the police force. Having completed my training in the RAF I never thought that I would have to go through it once again.

With the training school behind me, I was at least part way through my two years probationary period. My time now would be spent entirely on the Brighton streets. I had been posted to 'B' Division, the police station being in Wellington Road, which covered the eastern part of the town stretching from Lewes Road out to Longridge Avenue at Saltdean, northwards to cover Stanmer Park and Coldean as well as Moulescombe. This was a massive area compared with 'A' Division, which concentrated on the town centre.

The first couple of weeks or so was spent on the beat with the regular constable who showed you around, pointing out the important parts of it – that was, if you were lucky enough to be with a constable who was interested. Some of them were classed as 'uniform carriers' and had little interest in the job. I was pretty lucky as I only encountered a couple of this type.

Once this task was achieved you were on your own and would work on the beats generally considered not so busy. These in the main were the more boring beats. Worse still they were very hilly. They covered areas such as Southover Street and Albion Hill, Elm Grove from top to bottom and, of course, Bear Road. Another such beat covered Sutherland Road and the Race Hill.

On one particular weekday I was very lucky to have my beat switched. I was posted to St James Street fixed duty, 10am–6pm. I was pleased about this as it was a very busy area, very interesting and so time passed quickly. Once I booked on, however, I was told that my duty had been changed, and that I was to work '9' beat. I was pretty annoyed about this, but soon made my way to my box. It turned out to be a blessing in disguise.

Pc Keith Collins was posted to the St James's Street duty. At around 11am he was outside the bank at the corner of Madeira Place while money was being delivered and a raid took place. Pc Collins was badly hurt in this raid and suffered headaches for many years afterwards. The robbers escaped and to my knowledge they have never been caught.

Once you had completed your two years probationary period and passed out you were soon introduced to the busier beats. You could then ask to be posted to such as Traffic or CID, although generally you had to spend a few years pounding the beat first. As in many another job, there were those with 'blue eyes' who always seemed to get the cream and were pushed in front of others more deserving.

As my service panned out I have to say that I was very lucky and I was posted to a number of different departments at my request. I managed to serve in the dog section as a handler, I spent several years as a GP (General Purpose) driver and I worked in the communications department on radios and teleprinters.

I was elected as the divisional Federation representative, being elected each year for 12 years. I was also elected constables' secretary and deputy secretary of the Joint Branch Board. My Federation days were some of my happiest ones. I felt that at last I was in a position to do something for my colleagues.

Some officers in the Brighton Police enforced The Ways and Means Act. This was a mythical law employed for the sake of convenience. You might tell a habitual beggar, whom you haven't actually seen commit the offence, that the magistrates on the bench that week had a real downer on beggars, with prison being the punishment. Yes, it was a lie, but it did remove a problem to the public and, equally important, kept you on the beat instead of spending an hour or so writing a report at the police station.

The more conscientious officers were so passionately jealous of their beats that they looked after them better than the next man: anyone unwanted was chased away or arrested. With this in mind, some officers actually banned habitual drunks, beggars and vagabonds from their beats, and would issue summary justice to the offenders.

The most famous of them all during the 1950s and 1960s was Pc Basil Baverstock. He was a burly man, very experienced and as strong as an ox. He would have no truck with anyone who misbehaved. He acted fairly, but should you misbehave having once been warned, you were playing with dynamite.

He was a serving policeman during the early part of the war, but he was called up and served in the navy during the latter part of the war. Although his better years had passed, he still was one formidable guy. The beat best associated with him was West Street, one of the very busiest in the town centre (the police box was on the west side), and he ruled it with a rod of iron.

Pc Basil Baverstock (second left) with Pc Nick Kerry, on duty at a mayoral occasion in July 1963. [Author's collection]

Contrasting these days with modern day offers no real comparison. Police officers throughout the town tried to do the job as best they could, but society was very much different then and incidents occurred to which people simply shut their eyes. Today, I'm sure, the way that some policing was done in Brighton wouldn't be acceptable to some, but the town was a much safer place to be. Who is right and who is wrong? I firmly believe that the way policing was carried out was right for that time.

Finally, in February 1985, I was medically discharged from the force, having been on the sick list for 13 months and having had five operations linked to ulcerative colitis. That I am sure might warrant some sympathy, but the practical method of being discharged as a policeman was, in my opinion, pathetic and wrong.

One evening I was at home and continuing my recovery when a chief inspector and a sergeant knocked on my door. I invited them in and they explained their reason for coming to see me. I had been expecting them to call at any time. They served a paper on me, similar to serving a summons: if the person was touched with this official piece of paper, it was deemed to have been served. The chief inspector duly touched me with the paper, and after almost 27 years of service my police career was ended there and then.

I had been to police headquarters to be examined by the police surgeon, who had informed me that in his opinion I was not fit enough to continue my life in the police service, although I was a professional Police Federation official and was not actively involved in work in the front line of police work. Even to this day, I still smart when I recall the way I was forced to leave the service, a job I truly loved. In my mind, it was akin to being shown the back door instead of leaving by the front door with your head held high. I am not of course blaming the chief inspector: that was the procedure, and he was just carrying out orders. Leaving the service through being 'medically discharged' still leaves a nasty taste. Not everyone discharged in that way was genuine, sadly, but my case was, and I didn't want to leave.

If I lived my life all over again I wouldn't change my experience of the police for anything. I met some of the nicest and bravest people around, and I was lucky enough to meet and talk with some

Chief Superintendent Norman Cooper, pictured at Gatwick Airport when Sussex Police took over from the BAA Police in April 1975. [N. Cooper]

of the famous people of the time – Max Miller, John Lennon and the Beatles, Fiona Richmond and Johnny Morris of BBC fame. I was mixed up with the making of a few films like, 'Oh What a Lovely War,' and 'Stranger on the Shore'. I took part in the Mods and Rockers battles and was there when Her Majesty the Queen officially opened the new Sussex Police headquarters at Malling House, Lewes.

I also served with some of the best coppers around, people like Ray Bridger, Les Adlam, Joe Symons Peter Gear, Tony Bishop and Harold Green. There were the characters, too, such as 'Big George' Ickeringill, Bill Sansom and Jack Snipe.

There is always a danger when you name a select few that you leave out many others, and for that I apologise.

However, I must add one more name to this list – Norman Cooper, who was both an excellent copper and a character. He rose through the ranks to become the Chief Superintendent of Brighton, a rank equivalent of the Chief Constable of Brighton and one he thoroughly deserved. He was a tough sort of guy but very fair, a man whose side you wanted to be on and not against. Out of all the many policemen I knew and served with, he will always command my highest respect, as he does that of most of my former colleagues.

THE EARLY DAYS

The Brighton police force was in being from 1838 until 1967, a total life of 129 years.When it began Brighton was little more than a small fishing town, centred on North, East and West Streets, albeit one that was growing rapidly as a fashionable resort.

A rudimentary law and order system had been carried out by the High Constable and his assistants until 1810, when the Brighton Town Act authorised the Town Commissioners to appoint eight 'watchmen' to patrol the town at night. These men began work in January 1812, and another sixteen had been appointed by December 1815, by which time they had been given the title of constable. They were supplemented by patrols of the local inhabitants and one special constable.

In January 1821 the town was divided into eight beats or 'watch districts', each having a box for the watchman. In 1823 the force consisted of 16 men under the control of two superintendents. They wore top hats, black tailcoats and white trousers, and each was armed with a baton and a rattle – until 1829 they had to call out the hours and the weather.

In 1830 there was an attempt to establish a more permanent force, and a Mr. Pilbeam was appointed as chief officer. It proved largely ineffective, however, and the men were eventually dismissed.

The watchmen were first based at the old town hall in Market Street. This building had a very primitive custody room, generally known as the Black Hole. A new watch station was included in the plans when the present Town Hall was built between 1830 and 1832. Like the Black Hole it was situated in the basement of the building. (It would be condemned in 1929 by the Inspector of Constabularies but no action was taken, and it remained the police station until the new one was built in John Street some 36 years later.)

In 1838 members who were recruited to make up the first fully professional police force, replacing the watchmen, were based at the new town hall. They consisted of a chief constable, two superintendents, a night constable, three inspectors and 24 constables. The force soon started to grow, and in 1854 comprised ten officers and 51 constables. In that year it came under the control of the watch committee of the newly formed Brighton Borough Council. One of the first decisions the council made was to increase the size of the force by ten men and appoint a police surgeon and a plain-clothes detective.

In 1855 there was a change of uniform, the tailcoats being replaced by frock coats, while in 1868 the top hats were replaced with helmets. The force had by now swollen to a total of a hundred men, and further regular increases were made during the years that followed – to 150 by 1901, and so on.

In 1956 the force boasted a total of 256 officers and constables, and the total number of officers for the Brighton Borough Police Force in

Pc Charles King on Brighton beach, probably in the 1920s. [Connie King]

1967, on amalgamation with Sussex Police, was 415 men and women. (It wasn't until 1918 that the first women were appointed to the force, due in all probability to the outbreak of the First World War ,when the men were recruited for the armed forces.)

The first main police station for the town, as we have seen, was in the basement of the town hall. I always remember the few steps down, just inside the main door: they were very dangerous, and a number of the more violent prisoners seemed to fall down them.

There were other, small 'district' police stations located in various places

14

Pc Bill Riggs on point duty at the foot of West Street, 1937–1938. [Mrs Saunders]

around the town. The first was established in about 1857 at 64 St. James's Street, near the junction with Grafton Street. This building had a balustrade roof and urn decorations, and it can still be seen to this day. It remained a police station until 1885, when the premises moved to 2 Freshfield Road.

Others were established at the southern end of The Level (c.1865–1919.), 26 West Hill Road (c.1876–1919.) and at Preston Circus fire station, from 1903. As the town grew, district stations were required on the main London Road, and so two more were established. The first one at 18 Middle Road, Preston, was in place by 1871, and in 1888 another was established in Patcham, on the site now occupied by the Homeleigh Flats.

By 1888 the Rottingdean police station stood on the western side of the High Street between Marine Drive and West Street, but it was moved to a nearby house in West Street in 1916. A further police station was built in Rottingdean parish in the 1880s and 90s at 25 Riflebutt Road, Black Rock. (This road was completely demolished to make way for the new Marina Roads and complex)

In 1928 most district police stations were discontinued as the police box system was being adopted. These were special telephone call boxes whereby members of the public could call for help. However, the Rottingdean station continued until 1931. A new Rottingdean police station was opened in 1959 in a former bank building complete with the old bank safe at 53 Marine Drive. The building is still there, but it is a hardware shop now.

Collectors' items. Brighton's distinctive white police helmets were taken out of commission when the Sussex force was created on 1st January 1968. The picture shows storeman Bert Holcombe with the abandoned headgear, now said to be worth about £300 each. [Author's collection]

One of the things that made the Brighton Borough Police famous, as well as rather distinctive, was the issue of white helmets for constables and sergeants between 1933 and 1939. They were discontinued throughout the war years but re-issued again in 1952, and survived until the amalgamation at the end of 1967.

There was another innovation, too. In September 1933 the Brighton force became the first in the world to operate with personal radios, one way only from the central police station to the constable.

In 1947, a new sub-divisional police station was established in a number of large houses on the western side of Wellington Road. The official address was 21-27 Wellington Road and these premises were also used as the training school. At this time the town was divided into two sub-divisions, 'A' and 'B', the former based at the town hall and the latter at Wellington Road.

In 1965 a new police station was built in John Street, designed by borough engineer, Percy Billington, and officially opened on 27th

September by the then home secretary, Sir Frank Soskice. Once again the police were housed in one building. On amalgamation, on 1st January 1968, the new police station became the divisional headquarters for Brighton – now a division within the Sussex Police.

In 1956, the then chief constable, Captain Hutchinson, retired after a period of 23 years. He had been highly respected by the town dignitaries and enjoyed a very good relationship with the Brighton Watch Committee. He had been chief constable throughout the Second World War and had been privy to many wartime secrets appertaining to the Brighton area. He had gone a long way to modernising the force, which had reached a strength of 283 officers, including six policewomen, by the time he retired. He had the forethought to increase the police vehicle fleet, and at this time there were 15 cars and vans as well as five motorcycles. However, this was about to grow considerably during the next few years.

During the years from 1957 to 1963, while A.E. Rowsell was the chief constable, the strength of the force rose once again, mirroring the increase in the town's population: by the end of 1963 the force totalled 328 officers. This number gradually increased until at the time of the amalgamation on 1st January 1968 it had reached 402, comprising the chief constable and his assistant, five superintendents, four chief inspectors, 26 inspectors, 65

Above: Pc Laurie Harding demonstrates one of the world's first police pocket wireless set to the mayor of Brighton, Alderman Herbert Hone, in the 1930s. [Author's collection] Below: Contrasting sets of 1933 and 1967. They're rather smaller today.

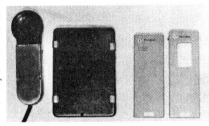

A policeman on point duty at Rottingdean crossroads in the early 1950s. It was a dangerous spot because of the speed of vehicles travelling west. [Author's collection]

sergeants, 271 male constables and 16 policewomen (including one inspector and one sergeant.) There were 13 vacancies at this time, which were not filled due to the impending amalgamation.

On the retirement of Mr. Rowsell his deputy, Bill Cavey, was promoted to chief constable. He was to be the last chief constable of the Brighton Borough Police Force. This man amazed me, as he knew every member of the force by name – quite an achievement, by any standards.

Brighton Police Fire Brigade

The police turned out with the town's fire escapes as well as with the volunteer brigade and the fire establishment. But because of a very serious fire in Queen's Road in 1880, an official police fire brigade was formed a year later. It was based at the town hall under Superintendent Thomas Gibbs.

The garages for the vehicles were built close to the town hall in Bartholomew's. However, following several serious fires in the town over a number of years it was re-organised and placed under

Inspector Victor La Croix, formerly with the volunteer brigade. He remained in charge until May 1921.

Following a very bad fire in December 1920 in West Street, at its junction with Duke Street, much criticism was levelled at this fire brigade and consequently a full-time and fully trained Corporation fire brigade was established at Preston Circus in May 1921. Under Chief Officer Stanley Thorpe the police and volunteer brigades were then disbanded. Thorpe remained the chief until 1929 when Charles Birch succeeded him – until 1955. Two further chiefs were appointed, Edmund Calvert (1955–1973) and Frank Furlong (1973–74.) The Brighton Fire Brigade was also subject to amalgamation.

The Police Museum

In May 2004 the then mayor, Councillor Mrs. Pat Drake, set up a committee to have a Brighton police museum in part of the old Brighton police station in the basement of the town hall. The committee scoured both Brighton and Lewes headquarters, and various police historical items were found. Some of these items had been displayed more than 40 years previous in the small police museum set up in Wellington Road police station and moved to John Street in 1965.

Former members of the force and their families donated items to the museum, and after a few setbacks – but with firm determination – it was officially opened on 4th May 2005. This was a real triumph for Pat Drake and her committee.

I would urge you to take time out and to visit this museum,which the committee has every intention of enlarging.

Within the police museum is a murder scene.
In 1844 the chief constable, Henry Solomon,
was interrogating a suspect when the man seized
a poker from the fireplace and struck him a fatal
blow to the head. Solomon's gravestone (right) is
in the Jewish cemetery off Ditchling Road.
[Author's collection]

TO JOIN OR NOT TO JOIN

During the early months of 1957 I was 21 years old and working for Sainsbury's at their branch in St. James's Street. There were a number of pleasant people working there at this time; and among them was Mrs. June Penn. She was married to PC Peter Penn, a serving Brighton policeman, and they lived in Rock Street, Kemp Town.

I started to get quite friendly with them, and it was June who suggested that I should give up my job with the company and join the Brighton Police. I had never had this occupation in my mind: I had a job, and I was wary about leaving the security of it. My father had advised me to secure employment and hang on to it, as it would see me through my working life.

Gradually, the idea grew, but I was still not sure about making the change or probably more to the point, imagining that I would really be able to do the job of a policeman. This was at a time when a certain sense of mystery surrounded the police. I had never been in contact with them before except on one occasion when one chased me for being noisy – well, that was all I could think it was for.

On several occasions over the next few months the suggestions continued and gradually the idea really started to grow: now I was becoming interested. As the weeks and months passed I asked Peter Penn a continual stream of questions. He was extremely helpful, and I spent many evenings at his home, eventually asking him what I had to do to join. I can recall sitting at home with the application forms on the table, pen poised – and then still not being sure if I should go ahead.

By this time almost a year had passed, and it was towards the end of March. I was still desperately arguing with myself whether or not I should go ahead, and then after one particularly bad day at the Sainsbury's branch I finally decided that it was time to give it a try. I filled in the forms and posted them to the town hall police station and waited for a reply. I was living in Dinapore Street at this time sharing an old house with my wife's grandparents, having two rooms on the first floor and sharing the kitchen.

One day there was a knock on the door and my wife's grandfather shouted up the stairs, 'It's for you, David!' I came downstairs to find a policeman standing there. I wasn't quite sure what to do or what he wanted. I invited him in and we went into the front room. My wife soon appeared with two cups of tea.

The policeman was Pc Michael Welch. I didn't know him at that time, but in later years we became good friends. (He had more success in his police career than I did, rising up through the ranks to become a superintendent. However, it's nice to say that he never changed – the same 'ole Michael'.) In later years he recalled that it was the first time he had interviewed someone wishing to join the police, having been given no specific instructions, only some vague guidelines from his sergeant. He asked me why I wanted to join, and I told him that I was in a rut at Sainsbury's and wasn't likely to rise any further. I believed that I would have better prospects within the police, and no doubt better pay. I asked about police accommodation as living where we were (two rooms upstairs and a shared kitchen) wasn't too satisfactory. I hadn't been married long then, and we had been gazumped on a flat in St.Lukes Road, that is why we had to live where we were.

Michael Welch interviewed me for the job. He retired as a superintendent. [M. Welch]

I recall that Michael and I had a lengthy discussion and then it was my wife's turn. In those days your wife had to be checked-out to make sure that she was of good character and a 'fit and proper person' to be a policeman's wife. Michael seemed to be happy with our answers and he reported back to say that I was a suitable candidate for the job. His report certainly did the trick. (So for all my former colleagues, who wondered how I was accepted, now you know that its Michael Welch's fault.)

It seemed a lifetime of waiting. Each day I hoped the postman would bring me some news about an interview or something positive. Eventually I received an invitation to attend the police station for an interview.

I can recall dressing up in my very best clothes and setting off in great trepidation on a sunny afternoon. I was quite a skinny guy in those days and about six feet tall: I knew that height meant a lot to becoming a policeman. I waited nervously in the outer room at the police station with two other young guys around my age. I knew that we were all in the same state of mind, all anxious to give of our best and to join the ranks. I seemed to have been waiting for a long time, my nerves all but shattered, but eventually was called in to see the superintendent, a large elderly man sitting behind a very tidy desk.

'Sit down,' he barked, indicating a chair in front of his desk.

This did nothing for my nerves. I could feel myself becoming a quivering wreck, and I knew that somehow I had to pull myself together. I felt very uncomfortable and had almost changed my mind while in the waiting room. I pinched my right leg so hard that the pain was almost unbearable, but I believe it did the trick as the pain took away my nervousness.

I was asked a few personal questions. How long had I been married? What sort of house did I live in? Had my wife, her family or my own family ever been in trouble or have a 'record'? A few more similar questions followed and then the question I had been dreading: 'Why do you want to be a policeman?' I recall mumbling something about I wanted to be involved with people and help the community in general.

'Yes, but you could do that without being a policeman,' he said.

By this time his attitude had softened, and I was at last beginning to feel a little easier, but was I giving the right answers? Was I doing enough to be accepted?

'I take it you know what the wages are?' he said.

'Yes, sir,' I replied. 'I think it's £10 a week.'

'No, that's not quite right. It's £9.10s, but you'll get a rent allowance on top of that. It will probably make it a little more that £10.'

A few other general questions followed, and he asked me how much notice I had to give Sainsbury's. I at last firmly believed that I had done enough to get the job.

'A week, sir,' I said in a much brighter and firmer voice. 'Just a week.'

'All right, then,' he said as he scribbled something down on his pad.

I expected him to say that I had got the job and sat there waiting. He looked up from his desk and said, 'What are you waiting for, lad?'

'Sorry, sir,' I said, 'I didn't realise you had finished.'

I got up, and I was about to leave through the door when he called out, 'We'll let you know.'

I left his office and as soon as I got outside I breathed a sigh of relief. I had found it quite an ordeal and hurried home to relate the events to the family.

A short while later an official looking letter arrived at home and I was half afraid of opening it. I feared a rejection, but to my surprise and delight I had been accepted, subject to a medical. Well, I was almost a policeman. The letter said that arrangements would be made for me to attend the Brighton General Hospital in Elm Grove for a chest X-ray and that I would also undergo a full medical examination by the police surgeon who had his surgery in Princes Street opposite the old register office.

I went to work the next morning feeling ten feet tall. I used to ride my cycle to work every day, and I must have thought about nothing else as I cycled along the busy roads through Brighton out to George Street, Hove. (I had been transferred to the Hove Branch of Sainsbury's by this time) I was dying to tell someone at work, but I knew that I mustn't say anything. I hadn't actually got the job, although I was pretty confident and it was looking pretty much as if I would get it.

I received further letters that gave me the times and dates for the medical side of the interview. I decided that I would have to have a sick day from work for the visit to the hospital and then tell the manager that I had a doctor's appointment. I first went to the hospital for the X-ray, having first phoned in 'sick', and a week or so later I attended the surgery. I went home knowing that I had done all right at the doctor's, as he had told me that I was fit and well. It now all hinged on the result of the X-ray that the doctor would receive and then send his report to the police. These were rather exciting days, although I didn't fully acknowledge it until some while later.

The day came when another official looking letter arrived on the doormat. This time I was feeling fairly confident, but there are always those little niggles at the back of your mind, that you may have somehow missed a small point whereby you wouldn't be accepted. I opened the letter with my fingers crossed, and there it was in black and white, with a starting date – I had been accepted; I was going to become a policeman. I was very excited. Now I was going to be somebody, someone who was looked up to in the community. I said to myself that I was going to be the best police-man that Brighton had ever had -- the very best.

I kept walking across the lounge imitating the policeman's measured walk, backwards and forwards and saying, 'I am going to be a policeman.' I was just so happy and excited.

I then took breath and suddenly realised the enormity of what I was about to do. It would be a complete change of lifestyle, and it was a daunting prospect. I would soon be changing my 9-to-5 type of job for one which would involve working shifts covering days, nights and weekends, something I had never done before. The doubts flood-ed back. Suppose I couldn't do this job: what would I do? But deep down I knew that I must give it a try. After all, everyone I knew convinced me that I could do it.

I signed the form, which was my acceptance for the job, and now there was no turning back. It had all happened so quickly. From the time I applied until the time I was accepted was a matter of a mere four or five weeks. I went to work with the view of giving a week's notice. but during the morning something happened which was to change things.

I was on the bacon counter, and in those days whole sides of bacon weighing 60 or 70 pounds were hung on large silver hooks above the shelves at the back of the counters for display. There were times when these sides of bacon were needed to be taken down, boned and cut up into rashers and joints for the customers. We tried to avoid having to do this during the times that the shop was open, but occasionally this couldn't be avoided. I was able, because of my height, to remove these sides of bacon from the display by myself.

This entailed dislodging them from the display rail by means of a long pole with a hook on one end. It was almost impossible to do this without both height and practice, and this morning proved to be one of those times.

I was very busy in the preparation department on the first floor of the shop, and I had a young strong lad working with me. I said to him, 'Go downstairs and find someone to help you get a couple of sides of bacon down from the display.' He went eagerly downstairs and returned with one of the smaller sides. He went back downstairs and a short time afterwards I heard some sort of commotion coming from the shop. I heard his voice and that of one of the under managers. Then the under manager came upstairs and started to rant and rave at me for allowing the lad to get the sides of bacon down on his own.

What had happened was that while getting down the second side of bacon, it slipped and fell off his shoulder and struck the leg of a female customer. It really wasn't such a big incident, but it shouldn't have happened nevertheless. I explained to the under manager that I had told the lad to get some help and didn't know that he hadn't. This failed to satisfy him, and he continued to rant and rave at me. It wasn't long before both our voices were raised, trying to out-shout each other. I told him to go away as he was acting like a kid. He then came up close to me in a threatening manner and I pushed him away. I think that's what he wanted me to do. I pushed him again and he made a comment about me.

I just saw red, and before I knew what was happening the small push and shove led to me striking him. To this day I can't understand why I wasn't suspended, but I wasn't. I was told however, that the area manager was coming to see me, and it was then that I told them that I would be leaving at the end of the week. The area manager, Mr. Phillips, never did come to see me, but I did run into him a few months later after I had joined the police and when he had parked his car on double yellow lines in Dorset Gardens outside the St James Street Sainsbury's branch. I took great delight in offering him some advice about where his car was parked.

The end of the week soon came, and at last the big adventure was about to start, although I first took a short holiday just to make a break between jobs. It was now halfway through June 1958, and I was soon due to attend the magistrates court at the town hall to be sworn in as Police Constable 127 Rowland.

My starting wages were £9.10s plus a rent allowance of another 25 shillings per week. My wages at Sainsbury's had been £10.10s. and so I had taken a drop in pay. The difference was that my position at Sainsbury's had been senior salesman – third in seniority in the shop with very little chance of going higher. To do this you had to be a 'Yes man', and that is something I wouldn't or couldn't be. In the police force I was, of course, starting at the bottom and could only go higher – or, rather, I couldn't go lower. I knew that to achieve a higher rank meant that exams had to be passed and that you weren't at the mercy of whether or not your face fitted.

At least, that's what I thought.

SWORN IN

My father's birthday was on the 25th June, and in 1958 he celebrated his 55th birthday. The following day I attended at the magistrates court at the town hall in Bartholomew's. I was very aware of the significance of this day. I was to swear that I would carry out the duties of a police officer in a fair way, and that I would always carry out my duty to the very best of my ability. I swore to obey the Official Secrets Act, holding my hand aloft and standing in front of the magistrates' bench, feeling their eyes burning through my body and following each and every word and movement I made. This ceremony lasted only a few minutes, and at the end of it the three magistrates alighted from their seats on the bench and with a smile, warmly shook my hand, welcoming me as a member of the Brighton Borough Police Force.

There were two of us being sworn in on this day. We left the court and returned to the police station. The sergeant then informed us that we could go across to the police canteen and take a short break, but that we should return not more than 15 minutes later. On our return we were briefed as to our next step. It was arranged for us to go to see Leo Stuckey, the force's clothier and that hopefully there might be something that fitted us. We were then allowed to go home with strict instructions to return at 'nine sharp' the following morning.

I walked home through the streets feeling very excited, thinking that I was now a policeman – or was I? I had forgotten that I hadn't yet been issued with my warrant card, the official document that proved to others that you were, indeed, a police officer. Still, at least I was beginning to *feel* like a policeman. I arrived home and soon had the kettle on for a cup of tea,relating the day's events to the family.

That night when I put out the light and closed my eyes, my thoughts were way ahead. Tomorrow I would have a uniform, which I hoped would fit . . . and then sleep took over.

The next morning I was up bright and early, reporting to the sergeant's office together with the other new chap, Donald Belgum. We were both sent to the police canteen for a coffee, the sergeant's comment as we left the room being, 'You'll need it!'

We were soon back and sitting in a pleasant room fitted with about half a dozen desks. The sergeant gave us a talk about the service, emphasizing the fact that it was a very proud and efficient force and that we had a lot to live up to. This theme continued throughout the short introduction to the history of Brighton police. He explained what we would be doing until we left for the training school.

It was now time for mid morning break, so once again we made our way across to the canteen – across the road from the town hall and where the CID was stationed. They had numerous offices on the first floor, and the canteen was in the basement. The canteen staff was quite a friendly bunch and always seemed to be smiling. This was a rare commodity with some of the police officers we came in contact with. There were many occasions when I felt a total outsider, being treated as though I wasn't there. I wondered what you had to do to be accepted by these people – they seemed to be a breed of their own.

I have to say that I was rather overawed with the whole concept of the job. I got talking to Donald Belgum, who told me that he had been a military policeman for a few years and would find the training easy as he had been through some rigorous exercises in the Army, where he told me that he had been in the SIB (Special Investigation Branch). He told me how hard it was going to be and that it was easy to fail the course if you didn't work hard right through it. This did absolutely nothing for my confidence, which was already rather wobbly.

Once again we went back and reported to the sergeant. He introduced us to Leo Stuckey – a civilian who had served within the force some years earlier. I went first, and he looked me up and down, getting an idea of the size of uniform. After a while he said, 'Skinny ain't yer? A 36 will fit you. Do you know your leg size?'

He wasn't very big in the world of tall policemen, but he was rather overwhelming and pretty bossy. I thought to myself, 'Don't talk to me like that', but I said nothing. He measured my leg size, ('Hmm, long legs!') and I was beginning to get a bit annoyed. Being a placid sort of person I said nothing, but more to the point I was very new and didn't want to say anything that might upset anyone. I was eventually given my uniform, and I just couldn't believe how much of it there was. Mr. Stuckey seemed to be emptying the clothing stores onto the long desk and giving it all to me.

'Is this all mine,' I asked, 'or is it between both of us?'

I knew as soon as I said it that I had made a terrible mistake. The sergeant said, 'Did you see him measure Pc Belgum?'

'No. I realise that it was a bit silly to ask the question, but there's a lot of uniform here.'

'You just wait, son,' he replied, 'till you're out on a cold, wet night. You'll be glad of it all and a bit more.'

Belgum was then issued with his, and we staggered away under the sheer weight of it all. Mr. Stuckey's parting remark was, 'Oh, you've still got to get your white helmets yet. They'll be in next week.'

We tried on our uniforms, and I was pleased to find that my tunic was too tight. This meant that I wasn't a puny 36 size after all, but a manly 38-inch. Just about everything else wasn't a bad fit, however. We were then told that we could take an hour for lunch ('No longer – be back sharp at two!' the sergeant shouted as we left the room). so we went over to the canteen and had a very nice meal at a subsidised price. We were still dressed in our civilian clothes and were therefore allowed to wander into the town. I went up North Street looking in the shops while Belgum met up with his girl friend.

During the afternoon we were shown around the various offices until about 3pm and were then given the rest of the day off. We were told that we were to be in uniform from the next day onwards from nine o'clock, and that this time it would be for a full day.

I was pretty hot and bothered by the time I got home, and I hadn't carried all my uniform then. The great coats were so heavy, and I could only imagine them wet. (In the years to come I would find out the answer to that question). I had a problem finding somewhere to keep my uniform because we were short of space in our very small accommodation.

The next morning, dressed up in my uniform for the very first time, I felt an utter comedian. I couldn't believe that I had to walk through the streets dressed like this. I was, of course, ready very early, and I kept glancing at the clock wishing it not to go around. I said my goodbyes to the family and strode off confidently along

Dinapore Street. I kept my eyes to the front, half hiding myself by pulling my helmet forward and down over my face. I thought no one would recognise me. I turned the corner into Richmond Street, started to walk down the hill and then stopped. I thought that if I carried on this way I would be on the main road, in Grand Parade, where it was very busy. Suppose someone stopped me. Suppose there was an accident. Suppose . . . I promptly turned around and made my way back up the hill and then through the back streets to Edward Street. I knew that I had to come into contact with the main road at some time, but I didn't want to walk along too much of it. I did make it to the town hall without any mishaps, and was certainly very relieved when I arrived.

When the sergeant greeted us with 'Good morning Pc Rowland and Pc Belgum' it really dawned on me for the very first time that I was now a policeman. 'Pc Rowland', I thought sounded pretty good. Pc Rowland. I said it over and over again to myself. Yes, it sounded good. I looked over at Pc Belgum and he looked very smart. His uniform fitted him very well and he looked as if he had been a policeman for years. I knew that I, on the other hand, looked an absolute sprog. There was no mistaking that I was new – very new. My mind flooded back to when I had first joined the RAF. How was it that some people looked very smart and professional in a new uniform while others looked a complete mess?

The sergeant told us a few more things about the police force and what was expected of us. He also told us what it would be like at the training school at Sandgate – and then, by way of an afterthought, he told us that we would be going this coming Sunday. I can't remember whether I was pleased or not, but I know I wasn't very happy at being away from home.

The one thing I will always remember about these few days just before going to training school was being told about learning things called 'definitions'. The sergeant told us that we would have to learn about 140 different definitions. These were very important as they were the basis of a lot of the decisions that we would have to make when we were on the beat. He said that we would be tested on them every week and that it was very important to learn them.

Pc Belgum said, 'Well, I'm lucky. I already know them.'

I wasn't too happy about learning this. I could see that this guy was going to be top of the class. Being very negative, I thought I would probably be at the bottom.

During the next few days we spent our time working in various offices within the police station complex. On the Friday we were issued with our railway warrants, given the day off on the Saturday and wished good luck by the sergeant.

I packed my bag and set off to the railway station en route to the training school at Sandgate. What was in store for me now?

TRAINING SCHOOL

At Brighton railway station, and with mixed emotions, I said my goodbyes, and soon the train was pulling out. I was starting out on quite a frustrating journey. It has always been the same in this country: the travel south-to-north and vice versa is fast and efficient but to travel west-to-east is a totally different story.

After some boring hours I eventually arrived at Ashford in Kent. I joined another train to Folkestone, then a short bus ride, and close on teatime I found myself in the main road in Sandgate, complete with a mountain of luggage. I walked the few yards to the entrance of a very large house set in its own grounds. The pathway wandered uphill for an eternity. I walked along a nice pathway, edged with trees and bushes. I thought to myself how pleasant this was and, apart from being away from home, I thought I was going to enjoy my stay here – until I passed a large tar macadam surface that reminded me of the old square-bashing areas in the RAF.

Passing-out parade at Sandgate Police College. Today the college is at Ashford, the former building serving as the headquarters of Saga. [P. Hooker]

I suddenly had an uncomfortable feeling. I recalled the sergeant at Brighton telling me that there would be some marching and drill, but I hadn't expected something like this. I reported in with a large number of young men from several different police forces from the region, which included the island of Jersey.

We were allocated our accommodation and I set about unpacking. I then joined the rest of the new recruits for supper. A training sergeant told us about the following mornings arrangements and the rest of the evening was ours. I went to bed but couldn't sleep for wondering over and over what the hell I was doing there. It was close on midnight before I closed my eyes, sleep coming as a blessing.

Up bright and early the next morning, I dressed in my brand new uniform and went downstairs. It was a glorious day and, once outside, I was amazed to see a large number of policemen wandering around, their heads stuck in small books. Every so often they looked up and mouthed something, then down would go their heads again into their little booklets. This would go on while they moved about the grounds. They were mainly walking on their own, but they were everywhere.

'What are they doing?' I asked a policeman standing nearby.

'Only learning their definitions,' he said.

I was astounded by this, and it dawned on me that tomorrow I would be joining the ranks for this weird practice.

Breakfast came and went, and at 9am I was sitting in a classroom with about 20 others, all new, all keen and willing to learn. We were treated to a welcoming speech that left us in no doubt what was in front of us for the next 13 weeks. It was made abundantly clear that we would work, work, work. We were expected to spend half the evening reading and learning about the day's lessons. We must also learn the booklet of definitions off by heart, so much so that we would know it word for word by the time the course was finished. That word 'definitions' seemed to haunt you: wherever you went it never seemed to be far away.

We were then introduced to our class tutor, a sergeant from one of the other forces. He would be our mentor, the one guy who would make or break us. He then told us about the college and the Sandgate area including, of course, the pubs. We were strongly warned that if anyone was involved in any sort of trouble in the town they would be sent back to their force and almost certainly sacked.

With that threat soundly ringing in our ears we went for our first break. Someone mentioned that we had to parade every morning in front of the officers. We had heard some loud noises with people shouting when we first went into the classroom, but, oh boy, I hoped not.

On return to the classroom we given our detailed itinerary for the whole course. There would be three exams – one after four weeks, and another after nine weeks and the final one just before the end of the course.

'You had better not come bottom,' the sergeant added with a smirk: there were two more classes in the same group as us and he didn't want a member of his group to disgrace him.

Possibly the biggest shock of the day was being told that we would be 'enjoying' square-bashing twice a week – three times or more if we weren't up to standard – as well as parades every morning, complete with inspections. We would also spend some time in the gym in an effort to get us fit. There would be cross-country running, too, although most of this would be on the beach.

However the worst news as far as I was concerned was to be told that there would be swimming, in an outdoor pool. This was terrible news for me, as I hated swimming. Worse still, I couldn't swim. I had contracted scabies as a child during the war, and as a result my legs were badly scarred and marked. The other children had made pretty nasty remarks about these, and so I never went swimming. Now, it would be worse, because I couldn't get out of it. I absolutely hated the water.

The following morning we found ourselves on the parade ground, lined up for our first inspection. We were very new and looked it, and I was pretty sure that we were going to have a tough time. We were to be inspected by the commandant on our first morning, and he would have a number of other officers with him. We were ordered to attention and then given the order, 'Produce appointments'. This meant that we had to pull our truncheon from our pocket and hold it up, at the same time removing our whistle from our tunic pocket and holding that up in the other hand.

The drill sergeant glanced down each line to ensure that we had our accoutrements in our hands. He then barked, 'Correct, sir!'

The commandant, Superintendent Brown from the Hastings Police Force, began his inspection. He asked your name and force and you had to shout it out. He stopped opposite me and asked the question. I shouted 'Rowland, sir, Brighton!' He nodded and moved on. He was picking up a number of the officers for long hair and dirty boots. The boots weren't dirty, just not quite as shiny as others, and the long hair would have been quite acceptable away from the training school. I had seen it all before, but we had been well briefed while at the town hall police station. I had spent a lot of time bulling my boots. and you could almost see your face in them. I had also made sure that I'd had a short haircut.

At the end of the parade the commandant welcomed us to the school and told us that he expected us to work very hard. The drill sergeant then took over

'You lot are a bloody shower, a disgrace to your uniform,' he barked. 'You can't march, you can't even line up straight. I'll tell you what, you will by the time you leave here – or else.'

I wasn't best pleased with the thought of what we were going to do. Instantly, I didn't like this guy, shouting and bawling about.

We were to find out about drill the very next day. We lined up outside the 'big house' and were marched down to the square. The drill sergeant was in his element, a very smart guy who had us marching up and down, up and down: left turn, right turn saluting from the front, saluting on the march. Forming up in three ranks, then two ranks open-order marching.

We were almost wetting ourselves with hidden laughter. We were an utter shambles, and the lines were anything but straight, one line merged into the other. The 'drill pig' was anything but pleased. He started to shout, calling us all the names under the sun. At times he was totally wrong, because we *did* know who our fathers were. We were brought to a halt, in a rather undignified manner, and he told us that we could have a five-minute break for a smoke. I was a smoker at this time and quickly lit up and enjoyed the pleasure, but I was only about halfway through my cigarette when we were told to put them out and line up.

At last the time came when we could go back to the classroom and start learning about the law, the reason we were there.

The next day, after the morning parade we went for our first session in the gym. The instructor was another sergeant, known 'affectionately' as 'Punchy' Wallace. Now this guy was so immersed in his gym work that it was quite unbelievable. He told us that his job was to get us fit, and that that was exactly what he was going to do. He said that he didn't want to see any slackers; otherwise the whole class would be given extra gym work.

We did a few exercises to warm up, and we were told that all three classes of new recruits were going for a cross-country run together. Well, apart from my dislike of swimming my next pet hate was cross-country running. I was not a guy with those sorts of interests, although I knew of course that I had to be fit to work as a policeman. There was certainly no getting out of it. We set off running down the winding pathway to the main road of Sandgate. It was rather nice to be out of the grounds for a short while. We ran along the pavements and then crossed the road and onto the beach. This soon sorted the men from the boys and I was soon being passed by almost everyone. I suddenly realised that if I wasn't careful I was going to be last, and I didn't want that as it might bring my name and face to the forefront of the instructor. I certainly didn't want to get on the wrong side of *him*. I needed to finish somewhere in the middle of the group, where I wouldn't be noticed. I started to work a bit harder and passed some of those who had recently overtaken me. I don't think that I was getting any faster, but that they were getting tired – those beach stones really took it out of you.

I managed to just about stagger back to the gym where Punchy was waiting, and I was very pleased to see others coming up the hill behind me. I have no idea where I came, but it wasn't last.

It wasn't long before we were back in the classroom, and funnily enough I felt more secure there. When the lessons ended for the day, it was back to learning those darn definitions. I teamed up with another guy and we went over them together, finding it a little easier to do it that way.

The week was now coming to a close, and we still had classes on Saturday mornings. Our weekend started at noon on the Saturday and we were then free until Monday morning, although I had to come back on Sunday afternoon because of the train times. I had a very quick lunch and made off to the railway station and home, arriving in Brighton at about 5pm. I would have to catch a train on Sunday at around 1pm, which meant that it was a long journey for such a short time at home.

The one thing I shall never forget about these journeys was the way back to the training school, sitting in the carriage by myself reciting these blooming definitions. We were tested on them during the first lesson on Monday mornings.

The second week saw us taken to Folkestone by coach to the open swimming pool. On every visit I was always the last one to get ready and the first to get out at the end of a lesson. At the beginning the class was divided into groups according to our swimming ability. There were just two of us who couldn't do it at all. We were told that we had to learn, and that ten yards was the minimum. Should we not achieve this mark, our police contracts would be terminated. I suppose that was inspiration enough: although it was very cold, and not very clean, I knew that I mustn't fail. I really tried my very best, although I hated every second of it, and I did manage to start to swim after a few visits to the pool.

The weeks at training school followed a similar pattern, with the class room law getting ever harder. To me it was like a massive jigsaw puzzle, learning the various Acts of Parliament, the Road Traffic Act, the Larceny Act, the Children and Young Persons Act, the different ages that children could or couldn't do something. How the heck, I wondered, was I going to learn all this?

We soon reached week four – exam week – that really brought the panic on. I found myself in a very negative mood. I seemed to be working hard but not getting anywhere and I sat the exam with great trepidation. I decided that I could only give it my best shot: if that wasn't good enough, then so be it.

I didn't see a lot of PC Belgum as he was in one of the other classes, but one evening he told me that he had a motorcycle and that if I would like to pay half the petrol money he would give me a lift to Brighton and pick me up and bring me back. He explained that it would not only be cheaper for both of us but, equally important, we would get there quicker than the train and have more time at home. That certainly appealed to me and so I agreed.

We had lunch and set off about 12.30 pm. He was wearing a crash helmet but I wasn't. We arrived at St. Peter's Church about 3.15 pm. That was already almost an extra two hours at home. We arranged to meet at the church at five o'clock on Sunday afternoon: another four hours at home and a saving in money.

Another week started and we were told to expect our exam results on the Wednesday. Immediately after lunch, and with a great flourish, they were read out. He called out the positions starting at the top. For a lengthening period my name wasn't called out: I wasn't second or third, fourth or even fifth. So it went on until, eventually, mine was called at 18th position. Oh, well! There were 21 people in our class, so at least I wasn't last.

The weekend came at last and Donald Belgum asked, 'What time did we get home last week?'

'At 3.15pm.'

'Right,' he said. 'We'll try to beat it this weekend.'

Sure enough we did, by five minutes. I have to say that I didn't really like it on the back of the motorcycle, but it was allowing me more time at home and that was important. The following week Belgum announced that he was going to try to get us home by 3pm, ten minutes off.

It was a nice sunny day and we set off at roughly the same time and headed our usual way towards the Pevensey Marshes. I thought we were going a little too fast and tried to tell him to slow up a bit but it was impossible while on the back of a motorbike. We got to the first part of the marshes and we were still going too fast. It really was so crazy, just to try to knock ten minutes off the time. We were now in a series of narrow bends, barely a car's width wide. Most of the time we were on the wrong side of the road, first one side then the other. I was now getting scared: it was beginning to feel suicidal, and I wondered if the guy had a death-wish! Going around one particular bend I was horrified to see a car coming around the bend towards us. I knew that there was no way we could avoid it. There was only a split second to make up your mind. I knew we couldn't avoid a crash, so I locked out my arms on the panniers and braced myself for what was about to happen. I wasn't wearing a helmet and in most motor-cycle accidents it was the pillion passenger who was hurt or killed.

There was an almighty crash and I was suddenly aware of leaving the pillion seat and flying through the air at a fast rate of knots. I saw the sky below me and then above me as I somersaulted over the whole length of the car and landed with a thump in the bushes. I lay there for some while, but I have no idea how long. I am not even sure if I lost consciousness or not. I do recall moving my legs and arms and feeling and stretching them.

I staggered to my feet and saw that there was no movement from anyone else. I went across the road and saw that there were two occupants in the car, both middle aged – a man and a woman. The woman had her arms around the man, who was the driver. He was quite badly cut, but I don't know what had caused his injuries. I went over to Donald Belgum, who was lying in the roadway, his crash helmet still on but his face covered in blood. He was in a terrible mess. I gently lifted off his helmet amid his groaning and tried to comfort him.

I then realised that we were all in great danger from any other vehicle that might come around the bend: the bends were blind because of the hedges on either side of the road. A car did come and the male driver got out and helped with the accident. After what seemed ages, but probably wasn't really very long, the ambulance and the police arrived. I believe that a second ambulance was called for the car driver and his wife. Together with Belgum I was taken to hospital in Ashford. Quite miraculously I had suffered nothing but shock and a few cuts and bruises.

Belgum had suffered a very bad gash in his forehead, caused by the lower part of his crash helmet. He was kept in hospital for the night. I was released from the hospital and caught a train from Ashford through to Brighton arriving around 7.30 pm. We certainly didn't beat any records that day, and neither would we after that. I decided that I would sooner go by train. Although slower, it was certainly a lot safer.

With the police on the scene, and especially because there were injuries as a result of the accident, we had to make statements as to the cause of the accident. They said that they would come to the hospital to interview us, but when we told them that we were policemen in training it was agreed that we would write them when we returned to the training school.

The policeman dealing with the accident had suggested that we should enlist some assistance from our tutors and then send the finished statements to their police station. It was strange writing about an accident – my first accident and my own.

The motorbike was a complete write-off. During the following 12 months Donald Belgum wrote off two more motorcycles but was uninjured on both occasions.

I can recall that it was all very embarrassing the following Monday when I had to relate the facts to the tutor. The statements were duly written and submitted and we never heard anything further about the incident. What a start to a police career!

The next few weeks up to the ninth week were similar to the previous ones except that now the actual learning about the law, with its numerous Acts of Parliament, was even more complicated. I was finding it tough going: the definitions were hard enough, let alone this complicated law. I studied hard and, looking back, I know it helped me, but at the time I was convinced that I would never be able to learn all the little ins and outs of the subject.

Meanwhile we were definitely getting better with the marching and the drill. It was certainly on a par with service drill, something I thought I had long left behind. However, the swimming wasn't going too well, and Punchy Wallace had twigged my little game of being rather slow in getting in. Now he tended to shout out, 'Pc Rowland, where are you, 'cos you're not in the pool?' Then, at the end of the lesson, I would be kept in while he asked me a question about something or other. I had by this time made up my mind that I had to learn how to swim properly, and I enlisted Punchy's help. I was then gradually getting the idea but still not yet actually swimming.

The ninth week arrived and evening homework took on a new dimension. I hardly went out, and had my nose stuck in my book for hours on end. At last Friday came, and with it the examination. I thought that it wasn't quite as bad as it might have been. I finished the questions with minutes to spare and left the room feeling relief. I just hope I had passed: I didn't want to repeat the work all over again.

Once again the weekend was spent at home, a much more relaxed one this time. I had by now got used to wearing my uniform and no longer felt that I stuck out like a sore thumb quite so much. Like all of the weekends it passed very quickly, and I was soon heading back to Sandgate, my definition book open, me mouthing the words. Glancing out of the train window, I thought that one day all this would have finished and I could lie in my own bed every night and not suffer the continual purgatory.

The following morning I made my way down to breakfast thinking that I hadn't been spoken to on parade for quite some while. This of course was tempting fate. I soon found myself on the parade ground for the morning inspection. There was a new officer taking it today, for every so often the staff were changed. I glanced along the line at this new guy with his flat hat, smart uniform and brown gloves. He had what I would describe as a weasel face and I straight away took a dislike to him, hoping that he wouldn't stop opposite me. What a hope! He moved along the line getting nearer all the time, and I could sense it – a gut feeling if you like. I just hoped that I knew the answer to the question he would ask me. He seemed to be stopping at every third policeman, and I had a quick count. Oh no, I was ninth away from the chap he was talking to now. Should I faint? the thought suddenly flashed through my mind. He grew nearer and nearer, now speaking to the guy three away from me to my right.

'Well, I've had a good run without being spoken to,' I thought. 'Can't always be lucky.'

Then he was standing right in front of me.

'Pc Rowland, sir, Brighton!' I shouted out.

'Where?'

'Brighton, sir. Brighton.'

'Oh yes,' he said. 'That's where they hold their hands behind them and say Thank you.'

'Sorry sir?' I retorted

'Didn't you lose your chief constable and a couple of CID men?' he asked me.

'I'm sorry, sir; I wasn't in the force then.'

He stared at me with a sickly grin, then moved on and stopped at a chap three places away.

We nicknamed him Mr. Three. I was rather upset about these comments and was surprised that a police inspector should have made such comments. He must have known that I was not a member of the force when that had happened.

We made our way to the classrooms after the parade ended and the immediate conversation centred around Mr. Three. The general impression was that most of the guys didn't much care for this new officer. The tutor then came in and we settled down awaiting the exam results. Once again the names were called according to the best results first, and once again many names had been called out before I heard mine: 17th this time. I had moved up one place! 'Better than going down a place,' I said to myself, covering the disappointment I felt. I really had believed that I would get a decent mark. Meanwhile Donald Belgum had once again got a very good score and second place.

The next two or three weeks were much about the same. Our drill was improving by leaps and bounds. We were told that it had to, because there would be a passing out parade in front of our families. I was able to swim four or five yards now – great, but still a long way to go. We were heading towards the end of the course, and I had enjoyed certain parts of it, such as the practical demonstrations where the instructors acted out as drivers at a road traffic accident and as shoplifters, with plenty of shouting and swearing making it all very real. I didn't enjoy the square-bashing, and certainly not the swimming, but I did realise that I had to learn everything.

We arrived at last to the final examination. It was very important to get a good mark and position in this one: it could determine whether your police career took off or floundered. We also had the swimming tests, the minimum pass being able to swim ten yards, and I was a bit off that yet. I would know the outcome of this test in just two days time.

The morning of the final examination dawned and the class appeared to feel a mingling of excitement and relief. Once again I found the test papers very fair. They weren't as hard as I had feared and I finished it within the allotted time. We then spent the rest of the morning with the drill sergeant, perfecting our skills. He never said that we were good, but I knew that we were – as he said, just prior to marching off – 'not bad'. In fact that was his way of saying that we were actually pretty good.

There would be one last rehearsal for our passing-out parade and then our wives and families would be here to watch us. Accommodation had been arranged in Sandgate, and during the evening of the last day there would be an end-of-course dance. However, I was now getting quite worked up about the swimming test, which was in the morning, and sleep was a bit late coming that night.

The morning arrived and I knew that it was a very important day and I must do my very best and with full concentration. The other members of the class knew of my predicament, and a number of them offered support and wished me well. The coach arrived and we were whisked down to the outside swimming pool in Folkestone I didn't hang about this morning, I quickly undressed and got straight in the pool. One of the guys who was a good swimmer took time out to help me and gave me a short swimming lesson.

One by one our class members were called for their test. and as each one passed my time was drawing ever closer. I was getting very nervous until my name was called. Ten yards was one width, and as I started from one side over to where Punchy was standing I could hear the encouraging voices saying, 'Come on, Dave, you're nearly there, come on!'

Punchy was shouting, 'Come on Rowland, you can do it. Push out with those arms!'

I was painfully slow, but I could see the other side getting closer. I continued to thrash about in the water like a demented porpoise, but somehow I was making progress. Nearer and nearer I got. I lost the rhythm on one occasion, but with more words of encouragement I regained the stroke and carried on. I was almost there but felt I was losing it – although I was working hard I wasn't going anywhere.

I then heard Punchy shout, 'My hand, my hand!

I saw that he had leant forward over the pool. I grabbed his hand and he pulled me to the side. I hadn't made it: I had just failed. I reckoned that I had made about nine and a half yards. I was now going to lose my job, all because I couldn't swim. I was pretty upset. It seemed so cruel, after all I had gone through, to lose it just one day before the course ended.

And then Punchy said, 'What's the matter, Rowland? You passed, didn't you? Ten yards that was all you had to do, and you did it.'

Yes, I had done it, and all of a sudden it was a pretty good day. I had done it – but with a lot of help from Punchy Wallis.

We set off in the coach, with everyone singing. That hadn't happened before. In the afternoon we gathered in the classroom for our final examination results. I had to get higher than 17th. If I managed that, I said to myself, then this day would go down as the best ever. The tutor started off by saying something like we had been the best course ever, we had worked the hardest of any course etc. (I'm sure that is said to every course that is about to leave.) He then started to give out the results. Once again my name wasn't called out near the beginning. More and more names were announced and still not mine. At last I was called out at number 16 – 16th out of 20. No, it wasn't really very good, but it was a further improvement. From 18th to 17th to 16th, I did go the right way.

Meanwhile Donald Belgum had once again come second, a very creditable achievement.

All that was left was the evening dance, to pack my case and then home – home for good this time. No more Sunday teatime railway journeys, long and boring as they were. Monday morning would see me as a trained member of the famous Brighton Borough Police Force.

Believe me, I was so proud.

THE ADVENTURE BEGINS

Monday morning, the course had finished and now I was to report to my police station. While I had been at Sandgate the postings had come through and I had been assigned to Brighton 'B' Division. The police station was situated in Wellington Road, and that was where I had to report at 9am sharp. Donald Belgum had been posted to 'A' Division at the town hall police station.

Dressed in my new, neatly pressed uniform and shiny boots I made my way through the streets from my home in Dinapore Street hoping that no one would stop me. I arrived early and without incident. The constable in the front office showed me into the waiting room and informed the duty sergeant. A few minutes later I was summoned to his office, where he told me about my duties during the next few days. I was told that I would be working a 9–5 day shift while I was being shown around the various beats. I was given a list of the beat box locations and told that I was to report to them at given times. Today however, I would be staying at the police station and be with the front office constable, who began to tell me of the numerous jobs that he did.

He told me that I could take a short break at 11am, sufficient time for a cup of coffee and a cigarette. As the time approached, the sergeant said the duty inspector wanted to see me. He told me about the saluting procedure, and very soon I was standing in front of the inspector, in his office.

He asked me a number of questions regarding my time at the training school, and in particular my examination results. He looked at me, glanced down at his desk and said, 'You didn't exactly set the place alight, did you?' He explained that I was lucky, as I had been posted to the best sub-division in the force and I would be expected to work hard, be extremely vigilant and to arrest lots of villains. I said that I would do my best.

'You're best had better be very good,' he came back, 'because we don't tolerate slackers'

The rest of the day passed without anything exciting happening, but I did feel rather unwanted as very few people spoke to me. The constable on the early shift went home at 2pm, being replaced by another. He was quite grumpy from the very start. He spoke to me very little, not being very happy working the late shift, which was 2–10pm.

He told me to write something in a book, and when I asked him for clarification on a particular point he made a big thing about showing me, remarking in a sarcastic manner, 'I thought you would have learned that at Sandgate'. I said 'No', to which he replied 'Oh leave it – I'll do it.' There was a frosty atmosphere for the remainder of the afternoon. This had the effect of making the time stretch on for what appeared to be hours.

I had been told to report to the duty sergeant before I went home. He told me to report at the police station the following morning, when I would then be going out on the beat. I gathered up my belongings and then left for home, rather pleased to be away from the bad atmosphere generated by the constable on the late shift in the front office.

The following morning found me reporting quite early and full of excitement. This was the day I was being let loose on the general public for the very first time – the day I had been waiting for ever since I joined more than four months ago. I just couldn't wait to get 'out there and at 'em'.

The Brighton force was divided into two sub-divisions, each divided into a number of beats. The boundary of the two divisions was roughly The Valley. Standing on the seafront with your back to the Palace Pier, the left hand was 'A' Division and stretched out to the Hove Boundary. The right hand side stretched out to Longridge Avenue, Saltdean and included Moulscoomb, Coldean, Woodingdean and Whitehawk. This was more of a rural area and covered a pretty large expanse.

The beats were covered in two ways: some were 16 hours while others were 24 hours. Two constables working 10am–6pm and from 6pm–2am covered the 16-hour beats. The constable on the adjoining beat would cover the area after 2am as well as his own beat. The 24-hour beats were worked by three constables working three 8-hour shifts: 6am–2pm, 2pm–10pm and 10pm–6am.

I was now on two years' probation, this being a period where you had to prove that you were made of the right stuff and show the chief constable that you could carry out the duties of a police officer in an efficient and responsible manner.

The chief constable at this time was Albert Rowsell OBE, MM. He had been the chief constable of Exeter, but had been appointed on an acting basis after the previous chief, Charles Ridge, and two CID officers had been arrested in July 1957. (They later appeared at the Old Bailey, charged with conspiracy.) He brought with him another senior officer from Exeter, William Cavey, who took over the responsibilities of the CID. Rowsell was appointed chief constable in July 1958, and he served until he was succeeded on 8th October 1963 by William Cavey – the 13th and last chief constable of the Brighton force.

On the second day after the end of my course I was told that I would be working 15 beat. This covered Lewes Road on the east side, the boundary being along Lewes Road, up Elm Grove to Totland Road, down to Hartington Road and back to Lewes Road. It also covered all the streets between these boundary areas.

I would be patrolling with a senior and experienced police constable, who would show me around the area, pointing out the important parts which had to have extra attention paid to them – post offices, banks and factories, vulnerable places that might get broken into. It was important that at night you checked on these premises, and in particular the safes, which were illuminated at night and could be seen through the windows.

I was taught that when on patrol you walked on the pavement's edge, close to the kerb, so that you wouldn't obstruct the pedestrians and you were in a good position to stop a vehicle should that be necessary. It all seemed very plausible, although I have never been sure if it was correct. Certainly quite an amount of money was found in the gutters over the years, as well as small pieces of jewellery and other items.

During my training school days I had been taught how to stop a vehicle, interview the driver and check the driving documents. This was very elementary stuff and very easy at the school but I was now about to do it for real. I waited until there was a large space between the approaching car and me. I had to be sure that he could see me as well as my signal. I was a little nervous at my first attempt but knew that I had to make a good job of it or I would be a laughing stock. I didn't want to start my career with that type of name. I marched smartly into the roadway and raised my hand, signalling the driver to stop, which he did. He looked at me quizzically, as much as to say, 'What have I done?' I bade him good morning and assured him that it was just a routine stop. I asked him for his driving documents, which he passed to me. My tutor constable was standing with me, showing me how to record the details in my pocket book. Once it was done, he told me that I had acted correctly and we moved on along the main Lewes Road towards the bottom of Bear Road.

This was a period long before personal radios. You had no contact with the police station or with the modern-day communications room. Various police boxes were situated at convenient positions dotted around the town. This was called the box system, and you had to be at specified boxes at certain times, which was roughly once every hour. The boxes were fitted with a desk for writing your reports and statements. A telephone was fitted in such a way that it could either be used from inside the box or from the outside, and it meant that members of the public could telephone the police station from them.

One such box was situated at the bottom of Hollingdean Road, and it contained a number of white coats for use when traffic points were in operation. These traffic points occurred mainly during the early morning and the early evening when the local factory workers made their way to or from work. I was soon to get a taste of this. We were stopped a few times and asked directions, and while patrolling in Hartington Road a woman complained to us about the local kids being a nuisance to her. I made my way back to the police station a little before 1pm for my lunch break. You were allowed 45 minutes for this break and you were expected not to extend the time or take advantage: disciplinary action could be taken against you if you did.

The lunch-break ended and I was put with the constable in the front office until 2pm, when I was put with another officer on Lewes Road again, but this time on the other side, the western side. This was no. 16 beat, and once again it was a hilly one. It stretched along Lewes road northwards to Hollingdean Road and then up to

Ditchling Road, following down to the Level and along Union Road and all the streets in between this outside area.

While on patrol you were 'visited' by the sergeant probably twice during your eight hours tour of duty and by the inspector once. This was part of their supervisory role, and it was the beat constable's job to report any problems to the sergeant and inspector during their visit. They then inspected your pocket book, checking it carefully and signing it, noting the time and date. Another feature of this regimented, outdated pastime was that when the inspector came to see you, you had to greet him with a smart salute and say, '16 beat all correct, sir.' This took no account of how long you had been on patrol. You might have been on duty barely half an hour and had certainly not been around your beat when the inspector met you, but you still said the same thing. Some years later the saluting was stopped, but not the silly 'Beat all correct' business.

We had one sergeant who always used the word 'duckie'. He would meet you on the beat and say, 'All right duckie?' This was all right by most of us, but an officer whose surname was Drake used to go mad. It wasn't long before a number of other, more senior constables also used the word towards him.

The following day I was to spend in the training school. Wellington Road housed the training school, as well as being the police station for operational duties, and we were to spend a day every fortnight there. The training officer was a Sgt Alec Tincknell, a military looking man who apparently stood no nonsense. I went there the following day with about a dozen other officers, all with under a year in service though at various stages of their probation. The more senior probationers were noticeably more confident. I was almost completely lost: I didn't know what time of day it was. At this stage of my service a lot of things were just a blur.

I took my seat at the back of the class, hoping that perhaps I wouldn't get noticed. What a hope! Sergeant Tincknell welcomed us new ones to the class and informed us that we were going to work as we had never worked before. He told us that as probationers we would be watched, checked and kicked up the backside at every opportunity. We had two years to pass through our probation, and the only way to do that was to work, work and then work some more.

We were expected to learn the various subjects studied each week at home when we were off duty and if we didn't it would show the next time here at training school. He left us in no doubt that this was not going to be a picnic.

Then the lessons started. It was basic law, and this is what we had been doing at Sandgate. I thought, What a waste of time – we know this. That was my first mistake, as towards the end of the lesson the class were asked questions. Sergeant Tincknell pointed to each one in turn, expecting the right answer. All of a sudden I wasn't feeling too sure: nerves began to get the better of me. I should know all the answers, but would I know the one that I was asked? As he came closer I felt myself begin to blush, convincing myself that I would get the question wrong. Eventually he came to me and asked me the question, a really simple one. I knew the answer, but for some stupid reason I didn't come out with it, giving a wrong one instead. He glared at me and asked someone else, who gave the right answer. I could feel my face burning and I felt an absolute fool. I believed he had made a mental note of my name, and that didn't please me.

Questions were posed at different times throughout the lessons as well as at the end of them. I was having a really bad day. Towards the end of the afternoon I hadn't been able to answer one question correctly, and I was fast becoming very unpopular with the sergeant. I was sure he was expecting me to get every question wrong, and I didn't disappoint him. At the end of the day he said, in front of the class, 'Rowland, in future you will sit in this seat' (indicating one of the front seats) 'and you will sit there until the end of your probation – that is, if you manage to complete it.'

That was very good for my morale! I did manage to complete my probation, somehow, and I did sit in the front seat in the classroom right to the end of it.

Over the next week or so I was shown around all the beats on 'B' Division, including those like Woodingdean, Rottingdean and Saltdean where you had to borrow a bicycle from the police station and ride to the various boxes. Time was allowed to get to and fro, but whether you arrived in time or not depended on the strength and direction of the wind. Whitehawk was also one of these cycle beats, but that wasn't too bad to get to.

A senior policeman called Brummie Roberts showed me around Whitehawk, and I was glad to be with him. This was a really rough and tough beat with enormous hooligan problems, and I was destined to spend quite a few months there before my probation would end.

At last I completed my short period of being shown around the beats, and then came the day when I was to be let loose on the general public on my own.

There was a rolling beat system over a six-week period. As a rule you would stay on the beat for that period and then change to another one for the next six weeks. There were also a number of spare constables who filled in when there was sickness, holidays, courses or training. The new constables were put on the less exciting, and perhaps best described as boring, beats. This didn't matter at first to a newly trained constable like me. I was out there, on my own -- crime fighting, or so I believed.

My very first beat was no. 14 on a 10am–6 pm shift. My box was in Elm Grove, opposite the Queen's Park Road junction. It was dark, small and not very comfortable.

This beat was one of the worst on the division, being hilly and countrified. The boundary followed a line up Elm Grove to the top, along Warren Road to the top of Wilson Avenue. It included the pig farms and allotments on the west side of Warren Road. The area then stretched along Freshfield Road past the side of the hospital and race-course and down to the junction of Down Terrace, along this road to Queen's Park Road and back to the police box.

We had to book on by telephone to the operator at Wellington Road a quarter of an hour before the start time, and I was at the box and booking on by twenty minutes to the hour. You had to be out on patrol at 10am sharp, unless you had a very good excuse. You might be legitimately held up by reports needing urgent attention, but it was always best to go out on time and show your face.

I had brought a lot of uniform with me on this first day. I had been advised always to take a topcoat, a raincoat and my meal for the day. I didn't have a car and so I had to travel everywhere by bus. I hung up my coat on a small hook and donned my raincoat, as the forecast was showers. There was a small electric fire in the box and a high stool to sit up at the desk. There were a number of shelves containing the information files and the different report forms. At the training school I had been given a list of the simple offences and I was expected to report people for these during my two-year probation period. This was all part of the training and would stand me in good stead as the years passed. They included such things as parking, two on a bicycle, a bicycle with no lights, begging and chimney fires. There were quite a number of other offences on the list, although this didn't include the more serious ones that I might encounter as my police career unfolded.

When you first arrived at work there were several things to do before starting your patrol, and that's why you had to report for duty 15 minutes before the appointed hour. There were, for example, 'daily informations' (DIs) to read: these informed you of duty changes as well as other pertinent news. Then there were 'crime Informations' (CIs). There was also a beat diary where you were to write down any useful information: important inquiries, statements that were required and any other information that officers coming on duty should know about.

This was after you had 'booked on' by ringing the telephone operator at Wellington Road police station. All officers booked on to the same operator. When you were a senior constable, one of the first things that you asked the operator was who the inspector and section sergeant were. There were some good sergeants but others weren't quite so nice – certainly not to probationary constables. There were other matters to attend to before commencing patrol, including keeping your pocket book up to date. Sergeants and inspectors checked them every day and sometimes twice a day. These were very important because they were used in court as primary evidence when you had to attend. Another important document was the Force Orders, which included a page or so about each individual beat. Towards the end of the tour of duty – in fact ten minutes before the end – there was a series of 'points'. These were situated at road junctions about a ten-minute walk from the beat box. It was important to be at these points as either the sergeant or the inspector was liable to be there, and if you weren't there at the appointed time you had to have a very good excuse or it was a discipline offence. No probationers wanted to fall foul of this particular rule. I used to open my pocket book at the last entry and draw a line beneath it. I then wrote in the date, the beat number and duty time. Lighting up time was also entered, and of course the location of the point for that day. Later, as I became more experienced, I left this part blank so that I had an excuse for not making the point, but you would only get away with it on one occasion: a second time would be too suspicious.

I completed all these tasks and knew that I had to be back in 40 minutes time as that was my first 'ring'. There was a list of times when you had to call the operator at Wellington Road. At night this was a check that you were safe and hadn't got into any sort of trouble. Should you not ring in on time when on night duty, a short time would elapse and then the operator would inform the inspector and a search party would be organised.

Ten o'clock came quickly, and although I still hadn't read everything I stepped outside – outside on a beat, on my own and in charge for the very first time. Whatever happened on this beat during the next eight hours would be my responsibility. The thought overawed me.What ever had I got myself into? But then I thought, 'Be positive'. I had managed to complete my course somehow, and now I kidded myself that I would know what to do should anything happen. Somehow or other I completed the tour of duty without a single incident, apart from a few people asking me the way. This beat was on the North section. Tomorrow I would be on 9 beat, which was on the South section, again from 10am until 6pm. The beat box was near the old Kemp Town railway station in Coalbrook Road.

I was still living in Dinapore Street at this time, and I arrived at the beat box in plenty of time, having walked up Albion Hill and through Queen's Park. This was quite a hilly climb when you had to carry so much uniform. I knew that once I qualified for a regular beat I could take my uniform and leave it in the police box for the duration of my time on the beat. I went through the same routine regarding reading the various orders and informations. I made a note of the beat boundary, which was another hilly one. It followed Freshfield road up to the top by the racecourse and down Queensway. It also included Eastern Road along to the hospital. I filled in my pocket book and I was ready to begin my patrol.

My first 'ring' was at 10.40am and so I decided to hang about Eastern Road, standing on the corner of Freshfield Road watching the traffic go by. I noticed that the traffic had somewhat slowed as it passed, and it took me a few minutes to realise that it was because of me standing there even though I hadn't done anything. I suppose that was the first time I realised my power.

It was soon time to return to the box to ring in, and as I reached the junction with Coalbrook Road I heard the screech of tyres and a crash. I knew in my mind what that sound meant. I had heard it before, but only at the training school. A whole collection of thoughts rushed through my head. What should I do? Run – in the opposite direction? I didn't really get any option because I heard a voice shouting in a rather loud voice, 'Officer, officer, there's been an accident and they want you.'

What these people didn't know was that I had never dealt with an accident before. I strode over to the scene with my measured walk, head held high and pretending I knew what I was doing. I'm sure that they had more confidence in me than I had in myself.

I frantically tried to remember what I had been taught. This was now a test of how much I had listened to the instructor. I glanced at both vehicles, asking, 'Is anyone hurt?'

'No,' replied several voices at once.

'Good,' I muttered to myself. 'That's something.'

It turned out to be a very simple accident, and I soon obtained the details I required. One car had driven away from the kerb, close to Mac's Cafe, without looking. The other car had been travelling along Coalbrook Road towards Sutherland Road. I reported the driver who had pulled away for driving without due care and attention and gave him an HO/RT1 – an official form for the production of his driving documents.

I had become so totally immersed in this accident, that I was reminded of my lateness to 'ring in' only by a blue flashing light. It came from inside the police box but flashed through the window in order for it to be seen. I hurried back to it and explained the reason for my lateness, the operator reminding me that I had to report the facts of the accident to the station officer in the front office at Wellington Road. I had made one or two minor mistakes, but overall

I seemed to have got it just about right and I was rather pleased with myself. I didn't know the location of the streets on this beat as I had done the previous day, but I was determined to learn them for the future.

The beat diary was one of the most important documents, and after each 'ring in' you wrote your route for the next hour so that if you were wanted by anyone, such as the sergeant or inspector, they would go to the box read your route and then walk it in the opposite direction: that way they would meet you somewhere along your route. On this occasion it was Sergeant Carter who was on his way, and we met in Sutherland Road. He had a reputation for not 'chasing' probationary constables. I was looking forward to meeting him, and when he said that we should return to the box, I wondered why.

He leant his bicycle against the side of it. He was quite large, ruddy faced and bereft of a smile, and he had the reputation of not being very helpful, but there was something about him that suggested that he was, on the whole, a jolly chap. I thought that perhaps all these stories I had heard were untrue or had been told just to frighten me. This was a trait with the older constables against the new ones. He said, 'I hear you've dealt with an accident. Is it your first? Let's hear all about it.'

I told him the details and together, we set it out. He roughed it out on a spare piece of paper for me to write it out in the correct fashion after he had gone. 'When you have finished it,' he said, 'mark it up for me, as I know all about it.'

He then left the box to meet one of the other beat policemen. I finished my shift and hurried home, eager to relate the story of the accident which to me, at this stage, was a pretty big job.

The following day I was on 10 beat, 2pm–10 pm and I was looking forward to it. It wasn't the best beat, but it was a good one as it covered Grand Parade and Edward Street, two very busy roads. I was also quite near to my home. I duly arrived at the box in plenty of time and began filling in my pocket book. Just before 2pm the early shift constable arrived. He was a large, bull-faced sort of guy, totally smile-less. I think his name was Derek. He shuffled into the box: it was almost impossible for two people to get into it because it was about the smallest one on the division.

I said Good afternoon.' He just made a sort of a grunting sound. I said, 'Is everything Ok?' 'Yeah', he said. I asked him, 'Is there anything special I should know about?' He replied, 'Such as what?' I said, 'Can you tell me something that I should know about on the beat – it's my first time on here.' He said, 'I'll tell you what, I had to find out myself – suggest you do the same thing.'

With that he booked off duty, gathered up his belongings and left the box. I thought he was one of the most miserable and unhelpful constables I had ever met. I didn't know it at the time, but he wasn't popular with anyone. A little later on I would meet another couple of guys like that, although not quite so ignorant and unhelpful.

I had quite a busy afternoon with traffic and the like. The beat was a very hilly one, working up to Queens Park Road, past Egremont Place to Edward Street and then right along Grand Parade with the second police box at St. Peter's Church. Later on I was called by a member of the public to a drunk in the Pavilion grounds, although this wasn't on my beat. The guy was staggering all over the place and swearing. I remembered that I had to note certain things about his manner and behaviour because these observations would be important in court during my evidence: my mind was racing back to training school again.

Without personal radios you had to rely on a lot of help from the public. I asked someone to ring the police and ask for a car to come as by this time I had arrested the drunken man. After what seemed a lifetime a police car arrived, the crew not too happy at putting a drunk in their car. The driver said, 'If he pisses himself, you can clear it up.' It dawned on me that calling a police car hadn't been one of my smarter moves. I should have requested the old van known then as the Black Maria. The drunk was put through the usual procedures: invariably they couldn't or wouldn't tell you anything about themselves, but the desk sergeant with enormous experience would know most of them because they were habitual drunks and were therefore often being arrested.

The desk sergeant was very helpful.

'Your first one, son?'

'Yes,' I replied.

'Nothing to it,' he continued. 'easy as pie. I'll just type this out and then you can charge him.'

I was quite chuffed. I had an arrest and I was about to charge him. That meant that the desk sergeant was happy with the procedure. I charged him a short while later for being drunk and incapable in the Pavilion grounds. The desk sergeant then explained to me the procedure about going to court the following morning.

I got home after the shift and started to learn my evidence. I went over and over it trying to learn the evidence parrot fashion. When I thought I had learnt it. I had my wife look at my pocket book and follow the evidence through as I recited it. I hadn't quite got it and so I continued to learn it. It was the practice that a constable giving evidence shouldn't refer to his pocket book. There was no real reason why you couldn't, except for the fact that if you did then the solicitor in court could ask to see your pocket book and possibly find all sorts of mistakes in it.

The following morning, all of a quiver, I continued to spend time learning my lines ready for the court case.

The procedure for attending court was that you reported to the police clerk who wrote in his book what time you had arrived, and after the court case you reported to him again that you had finished. The court appearance attracted overtime payments and some constables deliberately went out looking for drunks and simple offences that would end up in court the following morning. Should you be on night shift and arrest a drunk, you had to get up early and go to court. This attracted more money as it was classed as 'duty time': you would be back on duty within a prescribed time and extra pay was paid at a premium rate.

I reported to the clerk and was told that the drunks would be up first. Soon my name was called. I went to the witness box, my legs shaking like jelly. I felt that everyone was looking at me, and as I lifted my eyes I realised that they *were*. I stood to attention in the witness box and the clerk handed me the Bible and said, 'Say this after me.'

I did that and then I was on my own. 'At 3.45 pm . . .' I began, and I carried on to finish my evidence. The clerk turned to the guy in the dock and asked him if he had any questions and received a negative answer. The magistrate then tore into him, as he had appeared in court the previous day, and he received 14 days in prison as he was unable to pay the fine.

I was interested in getting into police accommodation, as in February 1959 my first son was born. I came home one day rather excited as I had been allocated a flat in Wellington Road, close to the police station and only just around the corner from my in-laws. We went to look at it and accepted it straight away, moving in a week or so later.

Soon afterwards I was posted to 15 beat, which was Lewes Road, east side. This again was one of the hilly beats, as it covered the area along Lewes Road, up Elm Grove to Totland Road, down Hartington Road and along to Bear Road. This beat also had traffic points on it. One of these was situated at the bottom of Bear Road, and at busy times (the morning and evening rush hours) you had to stand out in the centre of the road and control the traffic. You wore a white coat and gloves in order for the traffic to be able to see you.

On my first day I was with a Pc Drake, an experienced policeman. He said, 'I'll do the first half an hour. You can do the second one.'

Very soon the time came for my turn. I put on a spare white coat, which was kept in a nearby police box. I was sure in my mind that I would cause an accident, which would make me the laughing stock of Brighton Police. Pc Drake said to me, 'Remember, take your time, and if you're not sure of yourself, just stop all the traffic until you sort yourself out.'

With that advice ringing in my ears I boldly stepped into the road and took over from him. I was quite pleased, as I felt things were going well. In fact after a few minutes I was beginning to like it, and I completed my time without any mishaps. This was something else to talk about when I got home: I had often watched the policeman on point duty in Lewes Road, but never believed that one day I would be doing it at that very spot. I did it many times afterwards and I did really enjoy it – there was nothing like standing in the middle of Lewes Road at one minute past five on a cold evening with a very strong and cold wind blowing in to your face and the sight of hundreds of cars, motor cycles and pedal cycles coming from Allen West's and haring down the road towards you. It was like a tidal wave about to envelope you and you really did need strong nerves. The secret I found was to stop all other traffic and just let the Allen and West mob go on their merry way home. It was an incredible sight. Sadly, that's another thing of the past.

Soon after this time I was working a 6am–2pm duty on 15 beat. Our baby had had a particularly bad night and had woken me up a few times. I always set the alarm for 5am, so that I had time to get up, have breakfast and get ready for work. I only had a hundred yards to walk to the police station to book on: no problem – or so I thought.

On this particular morning I was awoken by the loud banging on my front door. I woke with a start, wondering what was going on. One glance at my clock, and I was in a panic: I had 'done it in'. The clock was showing 6.15am and late for work was a discipline offence. I told the guy knocking my door that I would dress and come straight in. My wife got up and made me a cup of tea while I got ready. I drank the tea, hurried along the road to work and arrived to find the sergeant waiting for me. I booked on and he asked why I was late. I explained the situation and he told me that I would have to see the inspector.

I was told off at length for being late and warned that it was my very last chance. I was also reminded that I was still on probation.

I booked off at 2pm and made my way home, tired and not very happy. My son was teething and he too was not very happy. I went to bed early that night after setting my alarm again for 5am. Again, I was woken up a couple of times due to the baby crying. The alarm must have gone off and, sleepily, I had inadvertently turned it off. Once again I was woken by the sound of someone banging on the front door.

'Oh no,' I cried, 'I've done it again! I've done it in!'

I went down to the front door and said I would be in as soon as possible. My wife got up and made me a cup of tea again. I really thought that this would be it – I'd been warned yesterday, and I firmly believed that I was going to get the sack. As a probationer you could be sacked straight away. The training officer's words came flooding back: '*If* you manage to complete it . . .'

I decided that as I was probably going to lose my job, I might as well stay at home and have my breakfast before I went to work. I ate it and walked calmly along the road to the police station. I booked on and was told to see the sergeant straight away. I went to his office and he went red with rage.

'Where the hell have you been? It's now past 7am and your beat has not been covered for an hour!'

He raged on a bit more before telling me to see the inspector, who gave me the same sort of treatment. As I was leaving he told me that I would appear before the superintendent later in the morning.

Now I was certain that I was going to lose my job. I ambled along Lewes Road, fully unhappy. Did they think I was deliberately late for work? Did they have a young baby who was teething? I bet not.

I returned to the police station around 9am for a break and was told to see the superintendent at ten. I was really worried as I loved this job and was so proud of it, as was my family, especially my father. I would be letting them all down.

It was almost ten when I reported to the inspector and was taken to Superintendent Beard's office. As soon as I saw him, the penny dropped. Just a couple of weeks or so ago I had been working on 6 beat, just for one shift. I had booked off and was walking up Upper Rock Gardens when I saw a big guy coming down the road. I had half recognised him and said 'Hello mate' in a friendly way. He looked at me, and although he didn't answer it was clear that he wasn't exactly my mate.

Oh dear! My mate just happened to be Superintendent Bob Beard. What with that and being late on two successive mornings, things certainly didn't look good for me.

I stood to attention while he read my report together with the one from the inspector. After a while he looked up at me and said, 'What else have you got to say?'

'Nothing, sir,' I replied.

He said, 'But you have been late twice in two days and today you didn't arrive until after 7am. You only live along the road.'

I was about to answer and tell him that I had stayed to eat my breakfast, when panic set in. If I got the sack I would lose my police flat and have nowhere to live. I thought better of saying anything about eating my breakfast and just said how sorry I was and that it wouldn't ever happen again.

He looked down at the reports again and suddenly said, 'How many alarm clocks do you have, Rowland?'

'One,' I replied.

'Well,' he said in a loud voice, 'then get another bugger and get it *today!*'

I left his office and the inspector said, 'You got away light, Rowland, but you'll work on two extra hours to make up for the time you've missed.'

That was the last time I was ever late. I bought another alarm clock that same day in a shop in Baker Street, although I could barely afford it. But I couldn't afford *not* to buy one, either.

WORKING MY BEAT

At last the day dawned when I was posted to my own beat. This was for a six-week period and I was to share the beat with two experienced policemen who I hoped would assist me with my questions about the law, application and the general procedures.

I had been advised earlier that it was better to put my questions to the senior constables than to ask my sergeant. The reasoning behind it was that if the questions were about something I should already have learned then the sergeant might regard you as thick and that would warrant 'extra attention'. This would mean almost certainly that he would spend much more time with you and ask dozens of questions which might lead to extra learning and writing at home.

It was customary when making your way to your appointed beat from your home and returning that you wore full uniform. It was drummed into you that you were a policeman 24 hours a day – even when you were asleep. (In later years you were allowed to go to work either in civilian clothes or, as most constables did, wear a civilian coat over your uniform.)

My first regular beat was no. 7. This was considered the second best beat on the division. The box was situated on the seafront at the bottom of Bloomsbury Place and next to a public telephone box. Each beat had another police box from where you could ring in to the operator from during your tour of duty. The other box for this beat was no. 9 beat box in Coalbrook Road. This posting made it quite a fair walk from my home in Wellington Road. It wasn't convenient to catch a bus, and so it was a walk up Islingword Road through Queen's Park, down Freshfield Road and on to the seafront. I was very excited at having my very own beat, and I was determined to show that I was more than capable of handling any problems.

It was now early in September 1959, and my first shift was 2pm–10pm, one that the majority of policemen disliked. Funnily enough though, I didn't. I was at the box very early, a little after 1.30pm. I hadn't known just how long the walk would take me, or if any members of the public would stop me and ask questions or that, worse, I would have to deal with some sort of incident. I hung up my coats and other parts of my uniform. This had been heavy to carry all that way, but at least I wouldn't now have to carry it any more until the end of the six-week period. I began to read the various orders, the diary and other beat notes that were pinned up. I checked on my ringing in times and the point I had to make for that day, writing all the information in my pocket book. I glanced back through the book and realised that it was a little sparse of offences. I knew that I must start booking a few people or I would have the sergeant and inspector on my tail. I waited until 1.45 pm before I booked on, because I didn't want any comments about me being at the box too early or being over keen, although of course I *was* a bit on the keen side.

I rang in and asked, who was the south section sergeant that afternoon, and to my dismay was told that it was Sgt George Spencer. The inspector was Mr. Gooch, and I was happy with that as he wasn't very strict as a rule, but Sergeant Spencer was a different kettle of fish. He had been my sergeant on a number of occasions over the past few months and I wasn't relishing the fact that he was now my regular section sergeant.

I was still attending the training school classes, and by this time had got to know the other young guys quite well. During the years that followed I became very friendly with Joe Symons (Constable 133), Ron Betteridge (169), Mickey Rance (150), Harold Green (277), Reg Keys (346), Tom Dyer (232) and Tony Thomas (200) I believe these numbers are correct, but when more sergeants were promoted they were given the next consecutive number, which meant that the constable holding that number was changed to a higher one.

All these officers had very similar qualities: they made very good and efficient policemen and exercised total fairness when dealing with the public. These were early days in our careers, and all of us found the theory side of the job quite difficult. To me personally the whole subject of the law seemed like a giant jigsaw puzzle, and I wondered if I would ever fill in all the pieces.

The early shift constable returned to the box after making his point, reporting that everything was quiet on the beat. He said that he had enjoyed his walk along the seafront and that there was

A police constable on duty at the bottom of Elm Grove. [J. Roberts/DTP Library]

'plenty of talent about'. Translated, that meant that there were plenty of girls wearing their short summery clothes.

I left the box sharp on time and walked along the seafront, keeping close to the kerb as I had been taught. I stopped at various road junctions, with head held high and pretending that I knew everything. One of the more difficult things to master on the beat was getting the distance and timing right. How long would it take me to walk around the route I had written in the diary only experience would teach me. I walked back to the box and rang in: the operator would pass on messages or tell you to ring the operations room if there was a call on your beat. There was nothing for me, so I set about writing in the next route I was going to take. I marked myself to patrol up Bloomsbury Place, then along St. George's Road to Bedford Street, returning along the seafront.

I was a smoker at this time, and one of the rules was that you could only smoke in the police box during your 45-minute meal break, not while you rang in and wrote out the patrol route. I had noticed that just about everyone did smoke while attending to these tasks, so I did just that – a rolled cigarette would last three visits to the box. I used to smoke about a third of the cigarette and then stub it out and put the remaining two thirds back in my cigarette tin. While I was having this quick smoke, I would open the window and leave the door open. Before I left the box, I would get a handful of papers and swish them to and fro in order to remove the smoke. I had a cigarette on this occasion, as it had been indicated that Sergeant Spencer wouldn't get to my beat before about 3.30pm.

I made my way up to St.Georges Road, a narrow but very busy street. It had a number of small shops on either side, where drivers used to stop on the yellow lines to visit the shops. There was a note on the board in the box about this problem, calling for 'extra attention' to be given to it. I was absolutely amazed when I reached this road: it was full of vehicles on yellow lines, both sides of the road. I thought, 'Gosh! What will happen if the sergeant arrives now?' I set about finding the drivers and getting them to move. I went from one end to the other and eventually managed to get them clear.

I stood at the bottom of College Place and positively beamed at my achievement. It was now that I wanted the sergeant to arrive and see what a wonderful job I had done. I stayed there for a few more minutes before I continued my patrol and walked westwards towards Bristol Road and then back to the box. I walked along Marine Parade and as I neared the box I saw a bicycle propped up against the side of the box and the door open. I knew immediately that it was the sergeant, and I wasn't looking forward to the meeting. I knocked on the open door on arrival and said the immortal words, 'No. 7 beat all correct, sergeant.'

He was sitting on the stool, and looked at me as if I had come from another planet.

'What!' he stormed. 'What. I've just been doing your work up there'. (Pointing towards St. George's Road). 'I've spent the last twenty minutes chasing away cars that were parked everywhere, even on the pavements.'

I started to give my explanation, but he broke in: 'This is your beat, not mine, and it's your job to see to the parking right through the centre and everywhere else on your beat. Look, you even have a note pinned up on the board in front of you. Did you read it?'

I could see that he wasn't interested in the fact that I had cleared the area, and we both knew that as soon as your back was turned it was full of vehicles all over again. He asked for my pocket book, turning back the pages slowly. I knew he was going to say something about it.

'Pc Rowland,' he said, 'this is pretty disgraceful, isn't it?'

'Yes, sergeant,' I said.

'You haven't had many jobs, have you? ' he continued. 'Do you walk around with your eyes closed? Everywhere you look there are offences. Why aren't you reporting them?'

'I don't know sergeant,' I replied feebly.

'Well, I think you're lazy. I shall be keeping an eye on you. I'll give you a booking in Marine Parade.'

He glanced at his watch, indicated a time, got on his bicycle and rode away. I was in shock and immediately thought, 'Blimey, he's a lot worse than I had first thought and I've got six weeks of this!'

I did manage to book a couple of motorists and attend to a domestic dispute in a flat in College Road. I also gave very good attention to the busy road where the sergeant had told me off. In the evening I was called to a rowdy group of young lads in Madeira Drive, and that was about the sum total of the day's incidents. I made my point at the correct time and went back to the box. I spoke to the night constable who was relieving me and related the story about Sergeant Spencer.

'Don't worry about him,' he said. 'He's a very good sergeant. He always chases probationers, but he's okay really.'

I left the box far from convinced. I thought about Sergeant Spencer all the way home.

The following day, I returned to the beat and was soon on patrol. I quickly made my way up to St.Georges Road; which was always referred to as 'The Centre'. The previous day's episode with Sergeant Spencer had certainly taught me something. As usual there was a line of cars stretching along the road, and I soon set about having them moved. I had been told by one of the friendlier policemen that one of the quickest ways of getting cars moved and with the least effort was to stand next to one of them and take your pocket book out of your tunic jacket. You had to make a big thing about it, glance down at the car number plate and pretend to write the number down in the book – the drivers would suddenly appear from out of the shops, apologising most profusely. I thought I would give it a try. I stood on the street corner for a short while and nothing happened. Not a single driver appeared. I went to a car roughly in the middle of the line and took out my book. I held it prominently in my hand and made a big thing about looking at the number plate, pretending to write it down in my book. I have never seen car drivers appear so quickly, apologising and driving away. I believe out of a dozen or more cars I only had to attend to two of them: the whole length of the road was completely clear. Now was the time for the sergeant to come, I thought – but that rarely happened.

I did see him later that afternoon. He looked at my pocket book, signed it, gave me a booking and cycled off towards Black Rock. He didn't say much to me, but at least I didn't get a telling off. I later had a visit from the duty inspector, and after attending to a few simple enquiries the shift ended.

The following week I was on the early shift. It meant starting at 6am but being at the box 15 minutes before. This was something new for me I had never had to get up so early for work on a regular basis. I set my alarm and got up without too much trouble. I was to enjoy the early shift throughout my career, and even after that at various other jobs. I patrolled my beat, walking along the seafront, thinking that I was getting paid to do this while holidaymakers had to pay for the privilege.

Every Thursday afternoon the force had a 'pay parade' at both the Wellington Road and Town Hall police stations. This was when your wages were paid, and you had to attend whether you were on duty or not. There would be an officer sitting behind a desk and you had to smartly march up and salute, stating your police number – mine being 127. He would hand you an envelope containing your wages, in cash. I can recall that on one occasion I called out my number and was given my envelope a little thicker than normal. I was off duty and was going shopping. I opened the envelope to find quite a lot more money than I would normally have received. I thought I had been paid overtime or some expenses that I had forgotten about. I was overjoyed with this amount of money.

When I arrived home and looked more closely at the wages envelope I found that the number on it was 217 and not 127. I had been given Pc David Redhead's wages by mistake. He later told me that he had quite a shock when he had a smaller amount of money than usual. It was soon sorted out.

The following week I started my 'night' week, which was a shift from 10pm–6am. I was never sure how I would cope working right through the night, but now I was about to find out. I had bought myself a decent torch with a strong beam. There were certain allowances paid on top of the basic wage, such as typewriter allowance if you used your own typewriter, but most constables wrote their reports by hand as I did. There was an allowance offset the cost of your torch batteries and another to cover the use of your own cycle on the named beats instead of borrowing one from the police station.

Working the night shift was quite different to working days. On nights the beat constable had to check every shop door twice during his shift, once before his allotted break (1.15–2am) and once after. Then there were so-called F's and U's (furnished and unoccupied premises where the occupier was away. An entry would be made in a book kept at the beat box and the night constable would check these premises twice during the night.

I finished the first night's duty and wearily made my way home. I had my breakfast and went to bed about 7.30am. I was soon asleep and then all too soon awake – just after 11am – and that would be the pattern throughout the week. In fact, that would be the pattern throughout my career, having very little sleep during the day. This lack of sleep made me quite touchy towards the end of the week. My children used to say, after I'd snapped at them: 'Watch out, the old man's on nights again!'

Close to the police box in Marine Parade was a nice hotel owned by Dora Bryan. The lounge was in the front of the building and on the ground floor. She employed a night porter who invited the beat constable in for a cup of tea at around 4am. This of course was very welcome, especially on a cold or wet night. The position of the lounge allowed me to watch the box, which was important for two reasons – to see the sergeant arrive or the blue light flash if I was needed.

A few weeks later I was on 6 beat, which most constables

considered the best of all. I was working the night shift, and there was what was generally termed a 'tea stop' on this beat, too. It was on the end of the Palace Pier, where the night watchman (in the right hand kiosk at the pier head when facing the pier) was very pleased to have the beat constable stop for a cuppa and a chat at 4am.

On this particular night it was misty and had been raining on and off all the time – one of those miserable nights that you firmly hoped wouldn't occur when you were on duty. The body is at its lowest ebb around 3am, a well-known fact which I didn't believe until I worked these shifts. I was walking on the south side of Madeira Drive and had to check the small boats lying overturned on the beach. People often slept rough here, and it was our job to check them as a number of criminals on the run had been caught this way. I had checked a number of boats without success and had returned to the pavement. As I continued walking westwards towards the Palace pier I saw a dark coloured car, without lights; drive around the Aquarium and into Madeira Drive and then stop.

Still being on probation, I was anxious to impress. Carefully watching the car, I made my way across the wide pavement to get into a position to raise my hand to stop it. I was very keen at this stage, but equally very green. Instead of continuing along the road, the car suddenly turned across the road and mounted the pavement. I was a little worried at this, but it occurred to me that I could report the driver for yet another offence. I hadn't come across this scenario at training school, so now I had to decide quite how to tackle it. Who were the occupants in the car? Were they yobs out for a bit of fun, or was there something more sinister about them?

The car stopped about 50 yards away from me, facing towards me. My thoughts were now racing. What was I about to face? I wasn't too scared, more puzzled: it felt a bit like being in a suspense film. All of a sudden the car lurched forward, gathering speed by the second and putting all of its lights on, blinding me. I had moved back across the pavement near to the railings, and I knew that I had to get out of the way, and quickly. I leapt over the railings onto the beach about six feet below, landing in a pile headfirst.

I heard the car screech to a halt and then, looking up, heard the sound of laughter. Two men appeared by the railings, pointing to me.

They were Pcs Geoff Green and Gordon Bartlett, the G.P. (general purpose) car crew.

'You all right, son?' one of them called.

'Yes,' I blurted out.

'Just having a little laugh. New, aren't you?'

I had hurt my ankle but I didn't intend to mention it. I made my way back up to the pavement, a little shaky but none the worse for wear. They drove off, still laughing, and I made my way to the Palace Pier for a welcome cup of tea. I was to learn as the years passed that policemen played many tricks and jokes on their colleagues. (One day, for example, an officer woke at home, to find his front garden set out as a cafe, with tables and chairs displayed in orderly fashion.) Well, I too had now been initiated into the Brighton Police Force. In years to come it would be my turn to do the initiations.

These tea stops were not really allowed, although the sergeants and inspectors knew that they went on: they had partaken of them long before I joined the force, and of course they knew where to find you if you were wanted. I recall working on the day shift on 9 Beat. I had had no calls to any incidents, no parking problems or disputes. I had called at a couple of houses in order to either take or arrange statements, but without success. The shift had really dragged. At one o'clock I sat in the box, ate my sandwiches, drank my flask of tea and then pretended to read the local orders and informations so that I could stay there a little longer. I managed to stay in the box for just on an hour instead of the allotted 45 minutes.

At about 3.30pm, after my prescribed ring in to the station, I made my way up Sutherland Road to Canning Street, where I had some friends from my Sainsbury's days. I knocked on the door and was met with the greeting, 'The kettle's on.' I went in and got settled in an armchair. The tea arrived with some cream biscuits.

We got into conversation and I suppose I had been there for about 15 minutes when my friend said, 'I think your sergeant is looking for you.' She could see through the window as she was sat facing it. I jumped about three feet in the air in a bit of a panic, my mind whizzing about trying to think of a good excuse. I said to my friend, 'Go and have a look and tell me when he's gone from the street.' She gave me the all-clear and I shot out of the house and went the opposite way, hurrying along the street. My problem was twofold: one, I knew that I shouldn't have been in the house drinking tea, and two, the sergeant was my friend Mr. Spencer.

I only had myself to blame, of course. I knew that others did it, but they had good and reliable excuses ready for an occasion such as this, having more experience than me. I had by now decided that my excuse was that I saw some kids misbehaving in an adjoining street and I had gone off my route to sort them out.

I made my way back to the box and as I turned the corner of Coalbrook Road I saw the tell-tale cycle propped against the police box. I gingerly entered, and the sergeant said nothing. This wasn't what I had expected. Perhaps he hadn't been looking for me after all. My fear started to fade. I said, '9 beat all correct, sergeant.'

'Is it?' he retorted 'How would you know? You haven't been on it. I followed the route that you wrote in the diary but couldn't find you. Where were you?'

'I was off my route as some kids were being troublesome in Rochester Street,' I said, 'and I went there to sort it out.'

'Oh, you got their details did you?'

'No, I didn't. They ran away.'

I knew darn well that he didn't believe me.

'You obviously chased them,' he said, 'as you've a couple of buttons undone on your coat.'

In my haste to leave the house in Canning Street I had forgotten to do up all my coat buttons.

'Son,' he said, 'when you have a cup of tea somewhere in future, don't do it when the sergeant is due.'

He left the box, mounted his cycle and rode away.

We had a few more bust-ups over the next few weeks. On one occasion I submitted a traffic accident report, which I felt I had dealt with quite well. I had taken my own statements and compiled the report entirely on my own. I was feeling quite pleased with it, and submitted it to the sergeants' office at Wellington Road.

I reported for duty the following day and in the folder I found my report addressed back to me. When there were problems with a report the sergeant would attach a note saying what was needed or what had to be changed. The note, signed by Sergeant Spencer, read simply 'Rewrite', with no other comments or remarks. Later, during my tour of duty, I sat down and wrote it out again, but I didn't know why I had to do it. I again submitted it back to Wellington Road. The next day there it was again, with 'Rewrite' on it in the sergeant's handwriting. I thought, 'Well, I'm not writing this out yet again.' He was my section sergeant today, so I waited for him to come round. He duly arrived and I said the usual silly words that the beat was okay.

'Any problems?' he asked.

I told him I wasn't very happy about my report bouncing back and forth. I didn't know why.

'Well, I thought you would see why,' he said. 'All the spelling mistakes, that's why.'

The conversation ended up in a right old row, and on that note we parted. I was pretty mad about all this, although I realised that my attitude might have gone down against me as a probationer.

Sergeant Spencer had a balding head and at times a very ruddy complexion. He had been a policeman for many years and was fast approaching his retirement. He was in a choir (in Patcham, I believe) and loved his singing. His nickname was Bacon Bonce, but this wasn't said in a nasty way or, of course, to his face.

At about 6pm that day he phoned me at the box to tell me to be at the box at a certain time as he was coming out to see me. I thought, 'Oh dear, this is it. I'm in trouble now, especially if he added up the various incidents during the past few weeks.' He cycled along Marine Parade towards me. He got off the cycle and came into the box.

'Right son,' he said, putting his arm around my shoulder. 'What's the matter? Let's sit down and sort it out, shall we?'

I told him what I thought, and he listened intently, explaining the probationer's situation and that it was imperative to get things right, straight from the start. He said he wanted to help all probationers. He left me to my thoughts as I wandered around my beat until time to go off duty and home.

After this incident Sergeant Spencer was the model sergeant to me, treating me like his son and helping me to learn a lot about report writing. He retired from the force in 1962, and to me he was a sad loss. (I had the pleasure of talking to him in July 2000, shortly after his 89th birthday, a little older but with just the same voice. Sadly he has since passed away. Although we didn't get on at first, he really was a wonderful policeman and great guy)

I recall another incident while I was working on 6 beat, which covered the seafront area, St. James Street and the south side of Edward Street plus all the streets in between. I had booked on duty in time for the night shift at 10pm. The weather was appalling, windy and with heavy rain – certainly not a night to be out. When I booked on I was told that Inspector Bourne was on that shift. Now, I wasn't a great fan of Inspector Bourne, a man of few words who could be a bit strict. I didn't think he possessed a sense of humour, either.

There was an officer working on St James Street, a fixed beat from 6pm until 2am. He was Pc Tom Dyer, a lovely fun guy. About 10.30pm we were both standing chatting in the doorway of the Sainsbury's shop on the corner of Dorset Gardens. We were both wearing our capes and I was smoking a cigarette. Wearing the cape, it was possible to hide your cigarette beneath it, even while you were walking along the street. We had been there about five minutes when a black police car pulled up opposite where we were. It was the inspector. We looked at each other and uttered a few words, knowing that we were in trouble by being together.

At this time the rain was really pouring down hard. Pc Dyer and I went out to the car, stopping on the driver's side and saluting smartly. Inspector Bourne wound down the window about two inches and said to Pc Dyer, 'I'll book you St. James Street.'

He said nothing to me but sat in the car looking straight ahead. I stood there getting wetter and wetter and after what seemed ages he said to me, 'Is that cigarette burning your fingers yet, Rowland? You had better put it out.'

'Yes sir,' I replied.

He then said, 'Why were you and Pc Dyer together?'

I stumbled over my words, not knowing what to say. I blurted out, that we had just met and were talking about crime. If I really thought Inspector Bourne was going to believe that, then I was a fool.

He said, 'Oh, crime – is that something you know about then? I'd call it idling and gossiping, wouldn't you?'

'Yes, sir'.

By this time I was soaked, the rain running down the back of my neck.

'I'll see you in Dorset Gardens,' he said.

He wound up his window the two inches and drove off up St James Street.

The following evening Tom Dyer and I were on duty again on the same beats. I said to Tom, 'I'll see you in Sainsbury's doorway at about 10.30pm.'

I said that the inspectors changed their route every night and so wouldn't get around to us until after midnight. The night again was quite unpleasant, raining but not as bad as the previous night. I was wearing my cape and as soon as I got to the Sainsbury 's doorway, I lit my cigarette. We both stood chatting when all of a sudden a black police car drew up. It was Inspector Bourne again. He hadn't changed his route and had caught us again together in the doorway. We both knew we were for it this time. I immediately dropped my cigarette and trod on it. We both walked sheepishly to the car and saluted. Inspector Bourne wound down the window a couple of inches and really tore us off a strip, reminding me in particular that I was still a probationer, and warning us both of the consequences should he ever catch us again.

He booked us and left. We parted with each of us walking down St. James Street on the opposite sides of the road. Never did we meet in that doorway again. We had been caught fair and square.

Inspector Eric Bourne went on to have a good police career, rising through the ranks until he became a chief superintendent and the divisional commander of Brighton. I got to know him a little better then due to my Federation involvements and found him to be a gentleman with a wonderful sense of humour. I invited him to my retirement 'do' at John Street in 1985 and reminded him of the incidents in St. James Street all those years ago.

CONSTABLE NORMAN BOLTON

Brighton recruited a police horse in June 1957, the first the force had had since 1939. Faithful was a 9-year-old dapple-grey gelding standing just over 16 hands, and his rider was Constable Norman Bolton, a very experienced horseman who had worked at his brother's racing stable at Lewes. He joined Brighton police in 1952 on completion of his national service, and very soon became a popular officer among the other constables.

Faithful was stabled at the rear of Wellington Road Police Station, easily accessible from Lewes Road, and many people used to visit him at the stables, either to just pat him or to bring him a few titbits.

Faithful came to Brighton from the Metropolitan Police, and Norman spent two weeks at the stables with him, getting acquainted,

Time for a snack: Faithful is given a titbit by Mrs Jeanette Robinson in Upper Lewes Road. [Mrs Sheila Bolton]

prior to his coming down to Brighton. With faithful came his best friend, a 5-week-old kitten named Boots, who was a tiny animal. They lived together in Faithful's stable, but a few weeks after the pair came to Brighton Faithful stood on the kitten's tail, which had to be amputated.

Faithful with his best friend, Boots the kitten, outside Wellington Road police station.
[Mrs Sheila Bolton]

Faithful and Norman were very popular and were often stopped while they were patrolling the town centre. The children loved to pat Faithful and make a fuss of him and he loved it too. On the days when their patrol included Upper Lewes Road, Faithful got very excited as he knew that was where Mrs. Jeannette Robinson lived and she would be waiting with his titbits. Mrs. Robinson was very fond of animals and simply loved Faithful. She had a 29-year-old tortoise as well as three cats, a parrot and a white rabbit.

Norman's duties were not just for show. He patrolled his area as efficiently as any foot officer working his beat. He took many prisoners, dealt with a number of traffic accidents and managed crowd control. One day he came across a traffic accident in which two vehicles had been slightly damaged. He was holding the horse's reins while trying to obtain the necessary details of the accident, and he asked Pc Peter Gear, who was on the beat, to hold the reins while he finished recording the details. At first Faithful stood perfectly still, but after a while he grew a little fidgety and stood on Pc Gear's foot. The pain was acute but, try as he might, he was unable extricate himself. It was suggested that this was Faithful's way of being friendly and the story goes that as Norman eventually rode away, the horse looked back at Pc Gear and moved his lips in a huge grin.

In January 1960 it was found that Faithful was unwell, and he was forced to take some sickness leave. A vet found that he was suffering from 'string-halt,' a complaint which makes the horse stamp its hind hooves. Concern began to grow over his health, but Norman and Faithful returned to patrol the streets of the town with the public totally unaware of the horse's illness.

Faithful was quietly retired after little more than two years as a member of Brighton Police, and his last days were spent on the farm at Wivelsfield Green owned by the Kemp Town MP David James. He developed cancer, a very rare disease in horses, and in May 1960 this wonderful and very popular horse was put to sleep.

Norman and his family were devastated. It was often said that Faithful had made more friends on the streets of Brighton in his two years than most people make in a lifetime.

On the 13th July 1960 Brighton Police had a new recruit, a horse called Kim. The horse officially joined the Brighton force in April, but his move was held up because he was required for duty at the wedding of Princess Margaret in London. This horse, like Faithful, came from the Metropolitan Police. Kim very soon became a favourite with the public.

Norman was a very good swimmer and captain of the Brighton Police life saving team which won many awards including district championships. A few years later. after taking over the riding of Kim, he was promoted to sergeant on 'A' Division and worked from the town hall. He was later promoted to inspector.

Norman died in 1974 at the age of 42 years, leaving a widow, Sheila, two sons aged 20 and 17 and twin 16-year old boys. The force was shocked and saddened by his death.

Norman Bolton with Kim.
[Mrs Sheila Bolton]

DICK CLAY'S STORY

This is the story of one of my former colleagues, Richard (Dick) Clay, a quiet, efficient and very likeable guy. He is also extremely modest and very brave, as the award of the BEM proves.

When Dick wrote this for me he was already 84 years old and not in the best of health, but his mind still very sharp, remembering things clearly that occurred during his wartime experiences (he spent more than six years in the Royal Navy during the Second World War) and, immediately afterwards, during his early days after joining the Brighton Borough Police Force.

After the war years he had originally returned to his pre-war job, an inside occupation, but soon found that he wanted to work outside: his war years on ships had whetted his appetite for it. He spent some time wondering what occupation he should follow before deciding on a career in the police service. The year was 1948.

He obtained his application forms from the police station in Bartholomews. It was practice to attend your local police station to have your height measured and so, as he lived in Hove with his wife Madge, he attended Hove police station, then situated in Norton Road, adjacent to Hove town hall:

❝ I was seen by the police station sergeant and duly measured.

'I can only make you five feet nine and a half inches son,' the sergeant said. 'You won't be able to get in at Brighton because they won't take anybody under five feet ten inches.'

Then he added: 'See how you get on, but if they don't want you, come back here and we'll have you.'

When I attended the interview at Brighton I was amazed to find that nobody said anything about my height at all. There were still two more tests to overcome before I was accepted as a Brighton police officer, the first being an interview by the chief constable, Captain Hutchinson, and the other being a medical examination by the police doctor, Dr. Hicks, who had his surgery in Princes Street. This was usually just a formality.

At the chief's interview he asked me a number of questions, in particular about the family and war service. I answered them without any bother, and then right out of the blue he asked me to spell a couple of words: yacht and diarrhoea. After I spelt these words correctly he then turned to me and said 'I don't usually take small men, but I'll give you a chance.'

I then found out that I had passed my medical examination and then I was in. I was a member of the Brighton Borough Police Force.

One of the many characters in the force at this time was a constable, Bob Burgess. He had a slight speech impediment which caused him to stutter. One day while on patrol he pointed out a small van to me in the vicinity of Park Crescent Place. He told me that the vehicle belonged to a notorious local villain who specialised in receiving stolen goods and selling them on the Black Market. He advised me to stop this vehicle if I ever saw it being driven, as it usually had a pile of stolen tins and packets of foodstuffs on board.

Ernie Waite. [G. Dean]

Funnily enough, I never did see the van being driven, but I later found out who the owner was. In later years he had a greengrocer's and poulterer's shop on the north side of New England Road, between Argyle Road and Campbell Road. His name was Ernie Waite, and in 1957 he would be prominent in the infamous Brighton police probe. At this time he had ditched his wife of many years and taken up with a young blonde called Jean Watson. They lived in one of the large houses in Preston Road between Dyke Road Drive and Lovers Walk.

The years went by and I found myself as a relief GP Driver before becoming a regular driver. Around this time I attended many accidents, and one day after a particularly serious one in which a man died, I decided that I would like to learn a little more about the art of first aid. Brighton Police had a nationwide reputation for having a great first aid team run by Inspector Maclean, and so I decided that I would join this team and therefore be coached by one of the best in the country. I duly learned a lot about the subject and won many competitions throughout the country. We had some wonderful people in this team, among them Bill Cowan, Ted Herrington, Derek Mann and John (Jack) Sole.

In 1950, probably the best year ever, our team won the coveted Grand Priors Trophy, which has been described as virtually the world championship. Quite an achievement! *"*

The next part of the story will have to be told by me, as Dick's modesty doesn't allow him to write about it. In 1959 he was teamed up with Peter Rubridge as a GP couple. They made many arrests together and on one occasion were called to an incident in which a man was armed with a firearm. Their actions that day were to earn them the British Empire Medal.

Pcs Clay (left) and Rubridge with their wives and children on the eastern lawns of the Royal Pavilion in October 1959 after being presented with their BEMs by the Lord Lieutenant of Sussex, The Duke of Norfolk. [Dick Clay]

The officers were patrolling in the London Road area when they saw a car reported to be stolen. Dick Clay, driving the car, pulled in front of it, and Peter Rubridge reached inside it to remove the ignition key. He heard a click and saw that the man was pointing an automatic pistol at his stomach.

The citation read that 'without hesitation both constables tackled the man, and after a fierce struggle removed him from the car and arrested him.'

It transpired that he was one of the most dangerous men in Cyprus, and that his gun was loaded with nine cartridges – one in the chamber ready for firing.

" One incident I remember I was working on GP with Derek Mann on nights. We were called to an all-night cafe on the seafront, where the Brighton Centre now stands. The cafe was called Montmartre, and we were told that a man was threatening the staff with a knife. Derek and I had a real struggle with him but eventually managed to handcuff him and take him to the police station.

We were just leaving the police station when the gaoler, Constable Dudeney, known as Dude, ran along to us and said 'Come back, quick!'

We returned to the cell block. Dude had looked through the spy hole in the cell door because the man continued to be violent after we locked him in. We peered in but couldn't see him.

Dude then said, 'He's up there,' indicating the top of the cell. Sure enough, he'd hanged himself. He'd ripped up strips of his shirt, stood on the toilet, tied strips around the back bars and his neck and then jumped off

Derek and I, both being first aiders, went immediately to his aid but it was too late: he'd broken his neck. I don't recall the actual outcome, but deaths in custody were always very unpleasant for everyone.

I recall one time when Brighton was invaded by the Mods and Rockers. On Easter Monday 1964 I was newly promoted to inspector and I was working the early shift (6am–2pm). I arrived at the Town Hall police station about 5.45am and managed to get home around two o'clock on the Tuesday morning.

We had had a lot of trouble in the town with these young people. There were 151 arrests and 149 'complaints against police'. Superintendent Denis Field was the officer in charge of investigating these complaints, although I did get involved with a few of them. One of them was from a 14-year-old boy from London with a fractured jaw allegedly caused by a policeman. His dad, it turned out, was the senior crime reporter on the *Daily Mirror*. It took over two years to complete the inquires on this particular complaint. *)*

Dick worked and studied hard during his police career and duly got his rewards, being promoted first as a sergeant and later as an Inspector, the rank he held when he retired.

Policemen on Dalton's Beach during the Mods & Rockers riots in 1964. (See also page 107.) [Brighton History Centre]

SOME PERSONAL THOUGHTS

When I applied to join Brighton Police I had certain perceived ideas of what the service was about. During my time at Sainsbury's I had witnessed, as well as been subjected to, some unfair treatment by management and heads of departments. In the first few instances I was very young (between 15 and 18 years old) and I was pretty green when it came to the skills of the working life. Then at the age of 18 I was forced to commit to two years National Service, and if there was anywhere rife with unfairness and almost total abuse of people in the 1950s it was certainly the armed forces. Most of the discipline had no logic to it: the idea was simply to commit you, quite simply, to blind obedience.

Having returned to my former employment at Sainsbury's, highly delighted that my National Service had come to an end, I was far from happy when the unfairness that I had experienced once again reared its ugly head. There was very little you could do about it and it was certainly not advisable to make an official complaint to the store manager. He would obviously back up his supervisors, and unless you wished to take it further, to the area manager, you were at a standstill. Make any type of complaint, no matter how serious, and you were destined never to further your career: you were tagged with a 'trouble-maker' label.

Having left Sainsbury's employment I expected fairer treatment in the police environment. That certainly was not the case during my initial training at Sandgate, nor to a degree during my two years' probation back in Brighton. The problem – same as always – was that you weren't really in a position to make a complaint to a senior officer, especially if the person was a sergeant with 15 or 20 years' service. You just had to grin and bear it. The police in those days was run on military lines, with lower ranks having to stand to attention and salute every inspector and above.

That was okay as far as discipline was concerned. I certainly accepted that – it was something that I fully expected and to a degree welcomed. However, you did expect to be treated fairly. The truth is that there were many occasions (after a serious incident, say) when an officer who deserved a commendation or something similar would be denied it just because his face didn't fit.

During the research for this book I have spoken to many former officers, both uniform and CID, and listening to their stories has convinced me that the unfairness was far more widespread than I first thought. On most occasions the officers were not looking for recognition, but it was very acceptable when it was given. One thinks of the BEMs awarded to Peter Rubridge and Dick Clay and of the Queen's Commendation for Brave Conduct won by Pcs Dave Thomas and Bernie Vousden for rescuing a woman who intended to throw herself from the top of a nine-story building in 1965. A year later another BEM was awarded to Pcs Johnny Lock and Nobby Clark for their conduct in the arrest of two men for armed robbery.

These officers, quite rightly were awarded these medals for outstanding bravery, but I know of an instance in which an officer disarmed a man holding a knife and threatening other policemen. yet failed even to be offered a simple thank-you from his immediate superiors. There have been other instances where information from serious burglaries has been given, leading to arrests and the recovery of property, and not one word of official thanks has been forthcoming, let alone a commendation.

On a personal note, together with another officer I attended an incident in the early hours of a Christmas morning, where a young woman was sitting on the other side of the safety fence at Black Rock, her legs dangling over the side of the cliff edge. We managed to pull her to safety. She ended up in hospital. Normal reports were submitted and then . . . not another word was said.

In many cases a lot depended on whether or not you were 'in' with your supervisors. This may sound like sour grapes, but I am just trying to emphasise the unfairness of the police service from time to time. Of course, we all know that in the real world many injustices are committed every minute of every hour of every day. Policemen in this country certainly don't go out looking for medals or other recognition – far from it – but they do expect to be treated fairly.

OXFORD STREET CROSSING

Many of us new constables, although married, had yet to have a family, and at the beginning of 1959 I was one of those in this position. The force was very helpful to young constables when their wives were in hospital having a baby. At Brighton General in Elm Grove mothers were confined to a stay of two weeks in those days, longer if there were any complications. The visiting hours were comparatively short compared with today – first two hours from six in the evening. Life on the beat made it very difficult to be able to visit your wife and new baby, but there were certain duties that the duty inspector would put you on if you wished. One of these was the Oxford Street crossing.

This crossing was in London Road at the junction with Oxford Street. It was a pedestrian crossing manned by two policemen from 9am–6pm. This was due to the amount of traffic and shoppers, as London Road was then a very popular area with plenty of well-known shops. You were often the butt of jokes from your colleagues if your name appeared on the sheet for duty on Oxford Street crossing.

However, this allowed you to make your hospital visits for the complete two hours. Otherwise, on the odd occasion you managed to worm your way into the hospital baby ward by saying that your duty clashed with visiting hours and a nice sister would allow you in for a few minutes.

In February 1959, when my first son was born, I found myself working the Oxford Street crossing. I have never really known if I enjoyed the experience or not – standing in the middle of London Road for two hours at a time and waving my arms about like a demented windmill, breathing in the bus and car fumes and disappearing in a massive crowd of pedestrians as they crossed both ways en masse. This was on top of being out in all weathers, which was particularly tough in the winter time. Quite often children would put sweets in your hand or in the pocket of the large white coat that you had to wear. These white coats appeared to be all one size and rarely fitted. Wearing one together with your white helmet in the summer, you looked like an early snowman.

Newspapers and magazines were other items that found their way into your coat pockets, while the one thing that we dreaded was that, while your hand was stretched out and you were concentrating on the traffic, some bright spark would deposit an ice cream and bid you good morning or afternoon with a beaming smile.

There were many occasions when you would stop an oncoming bus to enable the people to cross. As you stood aside, allowing the bus to continue, the driver would give his pedal an extra squeeze and pump out a massive, choking cloud of diesel fumes. When this happened, you made a mental note of the time, and on his next run along London Road you would stop him again, this time holding him up for as long as you could – sometimes waiting for a pedestrian to run part-way down Oxford Street or along London Road. When you let the bus go, you then held your breath, literally, so as not to take in the fumes.

You shared this place with your colleague, and when not on the crossing you would patrol London Road to help keep the traffic moving. Once your wife was out of hospital someone else would take your place. This would happen to me one more time: in February 1963, when my second son was born. By this time I was becoming an old hand, knew a few dodges and enjoyed the crossing duty a little more.

In later years constables working on the London Road beat and the Oxford Street crossing were given special dispensation to go to the police station in Wellington Road to have a cooked meal. The beat box for both of these duties was in Francis Street, near to one of the entrances to the Open Market, an extremely popular place for cheaper shopping. Constables going to the police station for their cooked meal had to book in to the operator and inform them that they were leaving their beat and going for their meal break of 45 minutes. They would then hurry across to the police station hoping to goodness that they were not stopped and asked questions. After their meal break they hurried back to the beat box to inform the operator that they were back on their beat.

The times that you rang in would be recorded and later checked by the sergeant to ensure that no one was away longer than one hour. It was all a bit of a rush. I used to take a few minutes less than

45 minutes to ensure that I was back on time, keeping my head down so that I didn't invite anyone to stop me. I must admit, though, that this wasn't always the case. I used to 'forget' to ring in when I was leaving my beat, and so there was no start time. This was however, something you could only do on the odd occasion or you would soon be rumbled by a sharp-eyed sergeant.

I believe that the best exponent of the crossing was Pc Bill Sansom, one of the force's true characters and one of its strongest individuals, too. (We shall meet him later.) His name appeared possibly more times than anyone on the crossing duty sheet – not only because he enjoyed this particular duty and was very good at it, but because his wife gave birth to several children.

Not Oxford Street, but the crossing at the foot of St James's Street. [Author's collection]

THE WHITEHAWK AREA

I was approaching the end of my probationary period in early 1960 when I was posted to No. 25 Beat, the Whitehawk estate and a neighbouring area which included, in contrast, Roedean School. Whitehawk and Moulscoomb were considered to be the two toughest areas to work on our division.

It was quite unusual for a constable still on probation to be posted to Whitehawk, as it was generally regarded as an area best suited to more experienced constables. I can recall that on hearing my posting, I was both excited and a little sceptical. I knew exactly what I was going into, having worked the area on the odd shift. I knew that if I did well it would go very much in my favour. If it didn't, well, I was only a probationer after all. In my simple mind I felt that I couldn't really lose.

Pc Freddy Deacon outside police box no. 44 in Manor Road during the 1960s. [Rosemary Deacon]

This beat necessitated the use of a bicycle and was a 24-hour beat, meaning that the area was permanently covered. The adjoining No. 8 beat was covered for 16 hours, with the box situated at the bottom of Arundel Road in an exposed position on the seafront. The policeman working on 25 beat would also cover 8 beat when its own policeman was not on duty.

The 25 beat box was situated between two police houses at the northern end of Findon Road. There was no rest on this beat as it was so busy. Apart from the large size of the area, it had more than its fair share of yobs and troublemakers and a vast number of 'F&U' houses, especially in the Roedean area. These properties had to be visited twice a night. There weren't too many shops on this beat, but they were quite widely spread over the area and these, too, had to be visited twice during your tour of duty. The two most important shops were the chemist and post office at the crossroads between Whitehawk Road and Roedean Road.

It depended which sergeant was on duty during the night shift, but certain ones liked you to be at the crossroads just before midnight. This saved them riding their bicycle up to the police box, reading your route in the diary and then trying to find you. It was an obvious advantage to you, because you knew that would be the only time you would see him. During the long, dark winter months they didn't come out to Whitehawk very often during the second half on the shift. When they did, they often told you to be at the No.8 police box on the seafront at a time they would be there.

Groups of youths would gather at the Broadway cafe in the Broadway, part of Whitehawk Road. We had strict instructions not to allow these groups of youths to congregate outside, as their presence was intimidating to passers-by. The accepted leader of the group at this time was a lad nicknamed Bimbo, although I never knew the reason for that. I must have been very lucky, as I never had any problems with them regarding misbehaving in front of me or failing to go back into the cafe when asked. The group at times numbered 15 or more, but there were usually around 10. They were often very rowdy, but only occasionally do I recall them being arrested for anything other than minor offences.

I was a little sceptical about being posted to this beat because of its reputation, but after a couple of weeks or so I got to like the beat very much. I met a number of very nice people, and found an incredible number of places where I was welcomed to have a cup of tea when following up 'police enquiries', whether it was for an unpaid fine, a statement or perhaps something else.

There was always a mountain of complaints, usually about loutish behaviour and nuisance from kids. However, that was offset in the summer when on the early turn you could make your way down to Marine Parade, lock your bicycle to the railings and take a walk along the undercliff breathing in the lovely, clean fresh air. I was along there one bright and sunny morning about 6.45am. It was low tide, with the rocks exposed and the sun reflected from the rock pools. I suppose I was dreaming of holidays when I was brought back to reality by someone shouting, 'Officer, officer!' I looked up and saw the local road sweeper waving his arms and shouting, 'Here officer, quick!'

He was pointing excitedly towards the rocks. I hurried to the spot and looked in the direction he was pointing. There was something that looked like a human body in the rock pool. Together we went onto the rocks and I saw an arm under the water and sticking out next to a large rock. I hesitated for a second, wondering what was the best cause of action. The body, if that's what it was, was certainly dead now. I needed some help, but in the meantime I decided to pull it out from the pool. I pulled on the arm and it came away from the rest of the body: it had clearly been there for some considerable time. We didn't have personal radios, so I asked the road cleaner to go back to the box and ask for my sergeant to attend the scene and for an ambulance to be called. This was one morning I wished I hadn't decided to walk along the undercliff for my first patrol. Had I not got involved the car crew might have got the call instead of me. However, it was on my beat and was therefore technically my responsibility.

The ambulance, the sergeant and then the inspector, soon joined me, and between us we managed to remove the remainder of the body. I believe it was identified some weeks later from dental records. I can still see it all in my mind. Some incidents never leave you. I remember one of the older policemen telling me soon after I joined that this would happen: 'Take it to the grave son, you will,' were his words. He was right.

One night I had cycled out to Roedean to check out a couple of 'F&U' properties. It was one of those nights when it wasn't fit to have your cat out. It was raining – not hard, but the stuff that wets you right through and chills you to the bone. The wind was whistling through the trees and moving them in an eerie fashion. As was usual when I went to the rear of these properties, I took the opportunity to light up and have a cigarette. I walked through the side gate and saw in the dim light that the fence was a few feet from a brick patio on my left hand side. It wasn't the practice to put your torch on straight away, and I was just about to do so when a cat I'd disturbed jumped from the fence across to the patio, catching my shoulder. I stood still, frozen to the spot. My heart must have missed a thousand beats as my neck went prickly. I dropped my cigarette and my torch and I was just so frightened that I really thought my life was about to end.

However, I soon regained my composure, picked up my torch and lit it straight away, flashing it everywhere. I couldn't have cared less at this stage if there was a burglar there or not. How I cursed that cat – I think I would have brained it had I caught it. I went around the back and shone my torch on the doors and windows, tried the patio door to make sure it was secured and then sat down on the steps. I lit up another cigarette and sat there smoking and trying to calm down. I then lit up another, and when I had finished that I went back to the front to resume my patrol.

This was the first night I had checked this property and the people would be away on holiday for a fortnight, which meant that I would not only check it again on this night but twice a night for the next two weeks. I never forgot that house and every time I went past it, the memories came flooding back – all this over a wretched cat. How pathetic are some of our big, brave Brighton policemen!

By the time my six weeks stint on this beat was coming to an end I found that I had made many friends, but the group of youths was becoming much larger, more offensive and at times more violent. One of the officers who worked the beat on odd occasions was badly assaulted, having his nose broken. More and more complaints were being received regarding hooliganism, intimidation and threats from the local gangs.

The senior officers had a conference and decided that they should act quickly and decisively, and my two colleagues and I were pulled off the beat and replaced by bigger and more experienced officers. The constables selected were Tony Bishop and Brummie Roberts, both brought up in Whitehawk and tough when required, and 'Big George' Ickeringill, recognised as the strongest constable in the force – a guy you didn't mess about with.

Within a week or so the estate was getting back to normal. The numbers of complaints were reduced and it became a much more relaxed area.

Big George started his week of nights on a Monday. He was very popular and already known to many of the residents. It was very easy to get into a habit when working a beat on a regular basis. George was no exception: every night just before midnight he would call at a small cafe in Whitehawk Road opposite the bus garage for a chat and a cup of tea. On the Friday night he leaned his cycle against the shop wall and went inside. He had done this on many occasions and thought nothing more about it. The bus drivers used the cafe at the end of their shift while waiting for a minibus to take them home, and George had got to know most of them.

Later on one of the drivers came in and said, 'No bike tonight then, George?'

'Outside,' he replied.

'It isn't,' the driver replied.

A charity walk by Brighton Police, with George Ickeringill on the far left of the picture. Peter Gear leads the way. [Mrs L. Ickeringill]

George went outside and, sure enough, the cycle was missing. He wasn't worried about the bike too much, as it was a double-crossbar police cycle and therefore quite distinctive. An excuse had to be found quickly, however, as the inspector would want answers– and soon. He made a few enquiries from the drivers, but without success. He informed the duty sergeant and inspector, saying that he had been called to the cafe as a result of a complaint. It was highly unlikely that they would believe him, but they wouldn't argue the point.

He completed the tour of duty without the pedal cycle and went home. The following night, when he reported for duty he was informed that it had been found in the tennis courts in East Brighton Park and had been returned to the police station. He started to make some enquiries, having his own punishment in mind for the culprits when he found out who they were. They had made a fool out of George, and it was his intention to make sure that it never happened again.

The following week he was working the late shift (2–10), and every day he called on people who he thought might be able to help him identify the persons responsible. Eventually these enquiries paid off, and he was given the names and addresses of three local youths. One lived in a street away from the main road, and before the week had finished George had caught up with him during the darkest part of the evening and meted out some 'Ickeringill advice'. This youth also confirmed the details of the other two youths involved. It would be another couple of weeks or so before George caught up with them, but they were given the same treatment. There would be no more taking of police pedal cycles, especially George's.

I suppose George was a hero to many of the constables, who marvelled at his strength and his general attitude towards his job, secretly wishing they were like him. I don't think anything ever frightened him. If it did, he never showed it. Fittingly perhaps, he was one of the country's top breeders of bloodhounds.

On another occasion when the gangs of roaming youths were at their most menacing, George had reason to talk to the leader called Bimbo in pretty strong terms. They were standing in Whitehawk Road outside the Whitehawk pub and the lad, not wanting to lose face in front of his mates, gave him some lip. One short sharp push and Bimbo fell over the small pub wall and found himself flat on his back. Infuriated, he got to his feet cursing George and challenging him to a fight over at the park. This wasn't a smart move. George, never one to duck a fight, duly met him at the arranged spot a few minutes later. It was like a scene from a film: the youths formed a circle and the fight began. It didn't last very long. George suffered a torn shirt, while the youth received one or two superficial injuries, and the loss of some of his blood – and his dignity in front of his mates. George had little trouble after that. Although the nuisance didn't come to an end, there was a great improvement overall.

I have already mentioned about the sergeants who always rode a police pedal cycle when visiting us on our beats. The inspector had the use of a car, and so you never knew when he would turn up. One night shift I was at the Whitehawk crossroads just before midnight to deal with a problem: local yobs were causing a disturbance on the last bus back to Whitehawk from Brighton town centre, and the bus company terminated the service at the crossroads instead of outside the bus garage in Whitehawk Road. It was decided that the beat man from 8 beat, the sergeant and I would meet the last bus in to lessen the chance of any trouble. The GP car often followed the bus , and so that was in attendance as well. With this show of force the trouble soon ended.

Another night we had some trouble with yobs who at first refused to leave the bus. We got them off, and as the bus was about to drive off they said they would get the driver as he left the bus garage after his shift. The driver happened to be my uncle, Jack Archer. I knew he would have no truck with them, as he could well look after himself. He was an ex-guardsman, tall and with a good build.

Five yobs ran up the road after the bus, and I wasn't sure whether or not they meant it. I was in time to see my uncle leaving the garage, walking down the slope towards the pavement. I didn't really see what happened, but one went down, quickly followed by another, and after a shout from a third, the rest ran off. The two who had gone down ruefully rubbed their chins, got up and followed their mates. There were no complaints from anyone, and that was the end of that incident.

Some while later, again working nights, I cycled out to Roedean Girls School. There had been some complaints from the school that a few of the girls had witnessed a 'peeping tom' around the school after dark. They were a bit concerned and asked for our help. I have to say that this was one type of offence that we had no time for. On this night I patrolled the grounds, and as I did so I found a dead rabbit by the roadside. It had been struck by a car and wasn't in too bad a state. I left the grounds and continued with my normal patrol, gradually making my way back to the police box for my 45-minute break. At about 4am I went back to the school and again saw the dead rabbit. I had brought a bag with me, and I put the rabbit in it and cycled back to the box, leaving it on the floor. I took it home at the end of my shift. We skinned and dressed it, and it made a lovely rabbit stew for the family.

In the police box there was the statutory small electric fire, which you were only allowed to have on when you were officially in the box writing reports or having your refreshment break. However, I used

A late 1960s view of Marine Drive and Black Rock, part of No. 25 beat. The Black Rock swimming pool on the left of the picture was closed in 1978 and Brighton Marina was later built under the cliffs.

to cheat as the time approached the 45-minute break. I would have my route passing the box about a quarter of an hour before my break, pop in and switch the fire on, then complete my route as written in the diary. By the time I got back to the box for my break it was nice and warm.

One very cold night there had been frequent snow flurries. Whitehawk always seemed to drop those extra degrees, especially on nights. I was frozen, and as usual I had put the fire on before starting my break. As well as a desk stool there was deckchair inside, and there was nothing better than stretching out in it to eat your sandwiches and drink your flask of tea or coffee. There was usually a selection of magazines, including a few from the 'top shelf', and so you were in heaven during your 45-minute break.

On this particular occasion, I wasn't only very cold but tired, too, and so with my sandwiches eaten and the delicious comfort of the deckchair I committed the cardinal sin of falling asleep. I awoke with a start some time later wondering where the heck I was. It was one of those times when it takes you a while to get accustomed to your surroundings. It turned out that I had been awoken by the smell of burning. Wisps of smoke rose inside in the box. I gave a good sniff and it was unmistakable – something was on fire. It was my trousers, the bottom of which had been too near the electric fire. They were badly scorched and had burned away, making the ends go into a jagged sort of pattern. I was glad I was wearing cycle clips as I could cover it up a bit. The smell of burning was very pungent, and filled the police box. I had to open the box door to get rid of it, although it was a freezing night.

Usually on nights, and after your meal break, you had to do 'box duties', which entailed cleaning and tidying it up – simply a quick sweep, a duster over the desk and shelves and so on. There was an allowance of fifteen minutes allotted for this task and on a cold or wet night this time was very acceptable.

I had overrun this, and I was very lucky. Not only had I narrowly avoided catching fire, but I was twenty minutes over my meal time and hadn't been caught.

BRIGHTON POLICEWOMEN

When I joined Brighton Police in 1958 there were only about eight policewomen working in the town. They were in their own department and were mainly used for any offences against women or children. Their work was thus more specialised than that of most male officers and they were trained to a very high standard.

Their hours were different, too. They worked 90 per cent of the time worked by the men, and their pay reflected this.

As the years passed their numbers grew, and by the time we amalgamated their numbers had doubled. Quite often their work took them into dangerous areas of crime. They often worked closely with the CID as they did with other squads set up for particular areas of crime.

In the late 1950s and early 60s the drugs problem started to rear its ugly head. They weren't the type of drugs popular today, but they nevertheless had a far-reaching effect on the body. The popular ones at this time were 'purple hearts', which gave the taker extra strength for a short period while they were under the influence. The policewomen were used extensively in pubs and clubs where these drugs were known to be circulating. Senior officers were often very pleased with the number of resulting arrests, firmly believing that they had the problem firmly under control. Little did they know that the drug scene would explode in the years to come, leading to the vast problems that every police force now encounters.

In the late 1960s and early 1970s policewomen began to work on the beats, and as the Federation representative in Brighton at the time I voiced my disapproval, bringing the dangers of this practice to the notice of the most senior officers. I had visions of policewomen being seriously assaulted and possibly raped. Fortunately my fears were totally dispelled, as neither of these problems occurred. So started a new era for the policewomen of Brighton and ,of course, for Sussex too. These days policewomen work the same as their male colleagues and are certainly on a par with them.

Who could have foreseen the changes that were going to befall the policewomen of today? Today's female police work bears little resemblance to that worked by the women way back in the 1950s.

For the record, the policewomen who were serving in Brighton on the day before amalgamation in December 1967 were Inspector Kate Morgan, Sergeant Kate Stemp (there was one vacancy for another sergeant) and constables S. Shiner, J. Oram, P. Warren, G. Lanfrachi, P. Wickens, C. Wiseman, J. Joyce, V. Edgington, C. Poulton, J. Southwell, D. Page, G. Tee, M. Bourton and S. Fowle.

One of Brighton's first policewomen, Gillian Tee, is see in a photograph taken outside John Street police station before leaving for a Wembley ice show. The male officers are (left to right) Tony Crawford, Brian Pronger, Brian Sheppard, the author, Peter Gear, David Thomas, Harold Green, Mick Sinden and Tommy Watts. [Author's collection]

BRIGHTON C.I.D.

During your first two years in the police force, and as part of your training, you had to spend some time in the C.I.D. They were based across the road from the town hall police station, just above the police canteen.

I was given a date to report there in civilian clothes, and I wasn't looking forward to it. It wasn't what I wanted to do. I was enjoying life on the streets.

At about 8.45am on a Monday morning I duly reported to the clerk (I believe his name was Colin Moore) and was shown into the main office. I stood around rather sheepishly as the C.I.D guys arrived for work. I think two of them just about nodded, to me while the remainder ignored me totally.

The duty detective inspector soon arrived and gave some sort of talk about a particular criminal, and soon everyone was getting about his business. I was spoken to by a sergeant and placed under the care of one of the detective constables. I got the impression that he wasn't best pleased with his lot.

I was given my duties for the next week or so and found that I was working 'split shifts'. That meant that I reported for work at 8.45am and worked until 1pm, when I could then go home. I would then return to work at 5.45pm and work then until 10pm. I have to say that I wasn't very pleased about this, as it meant a long day. I had no transport and would have to catch four buses a day to get to and from work. I was living at Thompson Road in Hollingdean then. I added the cost up in my head. It appeared that it was going to cost me extra money to be in the C.I.D.

The first thing my 'minder' told me was that he had some paper work to do and that my best course of action was to 'get lost'. I queried that, and he suggested that I lose myself in the canteen. He would come over for me when he was ready. I sat around for most of the morning, but he eventually turned up and we went out to make some inquiries.

We returned just before 1pm, and I was about to say goodbye when he informed me that I couldn't go home until the duty inspector said I could. He arrived at about five past one, spoke to various people about their particular inquires and then, at about 1.15pm, said we could go home. I asked the constable whether this happened every day and was told that it did. I went home, not very happy, but was back at the office on time at 5.45pm. I was soon assigned to another detective constable, and we went out to make some inquiries at addresses written down on a piece of paper.

We visited a few of these addresses in the Trafalgar Street area, and at about half past eight the constable said to me, 'Right, that's as far as we can go tonight with our inquiries. Now we have to visit a pub to meet one of my snouts.' (He meant an informer) I thought that this should be interesting. We wandered down Queen's Road and into one of the town centre pubs. The constable said, 'Your round,' indicating that I should buy him a drink. I ordered up two half-pints and we stood at the bar I assumed that we were waiting for the snout to arrive. The time went by, the constable glancing at his watch a couple of times. He bought a couple of half-pints, and still no one turned up.

Just then two other C.I.D guys arrived, and the constable said to me, 'Your shout'. Before I knew what was happening, I was buying four half-pints of beer. Still no one showed, and by this time the three guys were having a right laugh between them, telling jokes and laughing at them. I felt completely out of it and totally bored. This wasn't what I had joined the police force for.

At about 9.45 pm my companion said that it was time to get back to the office. We arrived just before 10pm and again waited for the duty inspector to give us permission to go home. At about five past ten he arrived and asked one or two of the officers about their day's work. He then told a joke, pathetic as it was, and everyone laughed. Reluctantly, I cracked my face, as it seemed the thing to do.

Around 10.20pm he allowed us to go home. By this time I had missed my bus to Hollingdean, and I was furious. I really objected to being kept unnecessarily at work. I got home close to eleven o'clock, tired out, although I had done nothing.

It was pretty obvious to me that not only did I not want to be in the C.I.D. but that they didn't want me there either. This was only the first day, and I was out of pocket despite going to work. I had spent what little money I had on drinks in a pub, something I wouldn't normally do. I was allowed some expenses, but far below those attained by the regular members of the C.I.D, and it certainly didn't cover my costs.

The remaining time I spent in the department roughly followed the same pattern ,although, one day I was called to the cell block where a number of young children aged around 12 or14 years had been held for shoplifting in the town centre. They were from the South London area and staying at a camp in Seaford, where they were selling the stuff

I was told that this was 'your job'. Whoopee: how exciting. I was taken over to the camp by an experienced detective constable to interview some of the kids there and to recover what property we could. We did get some of it back, and the kids admitted that they had bought it knowing that their friends had stolen it in Brighton. Although we didn't arrest all the kids, they were reported for the various theft offences we uncovered. We returned to the C.I.D office and I started the paperwork. It was long and at times complicated, but I did get some help and eventually we had it in some sort of order for the detective sergeant to check. In all, 32 kids were involved: some were fined while others were let off with a caution.

Another time I was allowed to deal with a couple of guys who had broken into their own gas/electricity meters and stolen the cash contents. All very big stuff, really.

Towards the end of my period I was interviewed by the detective chief inspector as to my suitability to become a CID officer. I was told to be at his office at a certain time. I knocked on his door and was invited in.

'Sit down,' he said, and I took a chair close to his desk.

The interview went something like this:

'Pc Rowland, you haven't exactly set the place on fire, have you?'

'No sir.'

'It's very difficult to judge you on your work, as you seem to have done very little.'

'Yes, sir.'

'Tell me what you enjoyed most about being in the department?'

'Do I have to be honest sir?'

'Yes.'

'Well, I didn't enjoy any of it. I wasn't allowed to do very much anyway. In fact not many people helped me.'

'That's hardly the attitude to take, Rowland, is it?'

'I'm trying to tell it as it appeared to me, sir.'

Finally he said, 'I can't find any reason to recommend that you become a detective, so you'll be returning to uniform as from this Monday.'

'Yes sir, thank you, thank you!' I replied, and so ended my brief, uninteresting career in the Brighton C.I.D.

Despite my own unhappy experience, I acknowledge that there were many very good young detective constables in the C.I.D over the years, as well as some good sergeants and inspectors. Others, however, really should have spent more time in the uniform branch.

Long after my time in the C.I.D there was a murder in the town and we were issued with the description of a man who was wanted for questioning. At this stage it was pretty obvious to us that the C.I.D knew who the guilty man was. A family member gave me some information which, as it happened, turned out to be of no use, although it looked promising at the time. He asked me to keep his name out of the limelight, which gave me a problem: what should I do with the information?. There were few CID officers that I would trust, but I did pass it on to one detective constable.

I forgot all about it until one afternoon, while I was at home in Woodingdean, a detective inspector and a detective constable appeared at my front door. I knew both of them and invited them in. I asked them if they wanted a cup of tea or something to drink, which they both declined. I thought that was rather strange.

The inspector said, 'Do you know why we're here?'

'No idea,' I replied.

The inspector then asked me about the information that I had received and passed on to the C.I.D.

Oh yes, I remember,' I said.

'Well I want to know who told you.'

'Oh no,' I said. 'I can't tell you that.'

The inspector and the constable spoke quietly and politely, trying to persuade me to give them the information they required. This went on for a while, until they became fed up. Then the tone changed, from a friendly attitude to one of real nastiness. The inspector got pretty mad, but I still stuck to my guns and refused to tell him who had told me. He then threatened me with my job, telling me that if I didn't tell him now, he would make sure that I was not a policeman by the end of the week.

I asked them to leave my house because there was nothing further to discuss. I was, of course, a bit worried about their threats . The following morning I was on early turn, and after briefing I asked to see my inspector, Ray Bridger. He was a man respected by our shift, and I told him what had happened the previous afternoon. He quite rightly said that it was a murder enquiry and it was my job to help as much as I could.

'But sit tight and see what happens,' he said. 'Come back here if it turns nasty again.'

I'm pleased to say that I never did hear anything more about it, but I learned a valuable lesson that day. Never again would I tell the C.I.D department anything that I had found out – absolutely nothing.

As can be seen, C.I.D. was definitely not my scene.

FIFTIES BRIGHTON

Here are some items from the 1950s found in local newspapers while I was researching other things.

POLICE BALL

Found in the *Brighton and Hove Herald*, dated Saturday November 2nd. 1957 and headed, 'Police ball was a sell-out':

The Brighton Police Ball was a complete sell-out again this year, and more than 1,500 people crowded the Dome and Corn Exchange last night to enjoy this big highlight of the local social scene.

A surprise guest: Chief Constable Rowsell.

There was one surprise guest – the temporary chief constable, Mr. A. Rowsell, who earlier had feared he would be too busy to attend.

The Mayor of Brighton (Alderman Charles Tyson) came to the Ball after attending an accountants' dinner, and the chairman of the watch committee (Councillor G. B. Baldwin) and the deputy chief constable (Superintendent T. Hill) were also present.

George Clouston rushed from the BBC television studios to conduct the Eric Robinson orchestra when they took over from Ken Lyon's band at 10 pm. Mr. Robinson was detained at a BBC 21st. Anniversary dinner in London, but he arrived later.

The Brighton Police Colours of blue and white were prominent in the decorations, and this year the flower-surrounded fountain at the south end of the Corn Exchange – looking sprucer, too, in its new coat of paint – was more attractive than ever.

The ball, organised by a Committee of the Police Athletic Association and Social Club, with Mr. Richard Geere the honorary secretary, was in aid of local charities.

POLICE RIFLE TEAM

Brighton Police were very proud of their rifle team, which won championships, medals and trophies both in this country and in Europe.

The rifle range was situated in the basement of Wellington Road police station. The club itself had a large membership and was blessed with some of the force's top shots who happily encouraged younger members. In 1957 the team enjoyed some of their best results, winning the Sussex Police league; coming second in the local league; and making it through to the semi-finals of the open national competition.

There was also a notable victory against a crack Brussels police team. The competition was held during the afternoon of Saturday 24th August 1957, and the home team was led by Superintendent Wally Friend. It was a tightly contested event, with Brighton running out winners by 1174–1170.

The individual Brighton scores (out of 200) were: John Harrison 199, Harry Feast 197 and John McIntosh 195.

With the match concluded, a dinner was held for the teams in the Royal Pavilion attended by the Mayor, Alderman Charles Tyson. An oak plaque with Brighton's coat of arms was presented to the Belgian team.

They next travelled to Brussels and returned triumphant by the huge margin of 100 points, 1179–1169. The range was situated at a site where, in the Second World War, German firing squads executed patriots after they had been caught and tortured.

The mayor of Brighton laid a wreath to Edith Cavel, who was shot by the Germans in 1915.

The top Brighton scorers were, Detective Constable Peter Andrews with 199; Gerry Openshaw, 198; and Sgt Harry Feast (captain) 197. In a special contest Pc Winter scored 195 out of 200.

POLICE COMMENDATIONS

During the summer of 1957 three Brighton police officers were presented with awards by the watch committee for bravery and efficiency.

In February of that year Detective Sergeant Alfred Dunford

disarmed a man carrying a loaded and cocked pistol. He was presented with a certificate of merit. It was a good week for the officer, who had joined the force in 1948, since he was also promoted to detective sergeant.

Two other certificates were presented by the committee chairman, Councillor G. B. Baldwin. One went to Pc Vernon Gray (an Australian) who on June 5th had rescued someone trying to commit suicide in the sea. The other was presented to Pc Ray Cross for his efficiency in arresting a burglar in Preston Street on 17th April.

Pc 109 Fred Deacon with a Morris Minor police car. [Rosemary Deacon]

MODS AND ROCKERS

The Mods and Rockers were two rival youth cultures prevalent during the early 1960s. It was a new social phenomenon – such rowdy public behaviour involving two large groups of youngsters was virtually unheard of until then.

The groups were totally different in their dress and modes of transport. The Mods were neatly dressed with short haircuts and rode motor scooters, which were invariably covered in badges and lights. The Rockers, on the other hand, were dressed in leather, many having long hair, and they rode various types of motorcycle. Most were between 16 and 18 years of age, with very few over the age of 20. The Mods would gather on street corners in groups of six or so, while the Rockers tended to be seen sometimes in twos and threes but mostly on their own. This invited trouble, but as they were on more powerful machines they often managed to get away.

Deckchairs fly on the Aquarium sun terrace.

During the Easter Bank Holiday in 1964 hundreds descended on Margate, which they turned into a battlefield, and some also came to Brighton. The police struggled to maintain law and order and called urgently for reserves from surrounding forces. A large contingent from the Metropolitan Police was bused into the town. Local and national newspapers were full of pictures and stories telling how the two groups 'tore up' the town, bringing fear and mayhem.

The weekends between Easter and the May bank holiday were fairly quiet, but rumours began to grow that the next target for the Mods and Rockers would be Brighton. Police intelligence was quite poor in those days compared with today, but the early rumours appeared to be justified. The chief constable, Bill Cavey, called a meeting with superintendents Bob Beard, Norman Custance and Alan Probyn. Where should they shepherd the youngsters? If they were kept to the seafront area, beach stones could be used as ammunition. If they were allowed to wander through the town centre the damage might run to many thousands of pounds. Other meetings were arranged involving the various departments, including C.I.D. and Traffic, with officers putting up ideas and suggestions. One of the biggest problems for the Margate police had been the lack of sufficient transport. After the Bank Holiday, moreover, they had many of their police vehicles damaged and off the road: normal patrols were difficult to maintain.

Several further meetings were arranged and again included officers from the various police departments, including CID and Traffic. The force was on something like a war footing. Senior members of the town corporation, including the waterworks, also had their say. More and more information was being gathered, and collecting it almost became an obsession.

As the Bank holiday got closer the organising went up a gear, and all officers were briefed daily as to what they were expected to do, including the possibility of working long hours with no time off – all leave days were cancelled to give maximum police cover for the whole weekend. One fact that surprised many people, including police officers, was the water board giving up their vehicles for police use. This offer greatly increased the numbers of vehicles available to ferry police officers to various trouble spots.

The water board vehicles were driven to the police radio station at Cranbrook in Kent by officers of the Traffic Division and were fitted with the Brighton Police radio frequency. On the day these vehicles were to prove invaluable, totally fooling Mods and Rockers who never expected a dozen policemen to jump out of the back of a blue corporation waterworks lorry.

As the bank holiday weekend dawned everyone knew exactly what to expect and what to do. It was a strange feeling. Without any discussion everyone was determined that these troublemakers would not destroy our town or frighten our visitors. The order went out to be very firm but fair, and to arrest anyone committing any offences, however small. We knew that many of them would fill the cells at the town hall police station – or 'battle headquarters' as it was known in a throw-back to the war years.

On Friday 15th May, the start of the Bank Holiday weekend, the Traffic Division set up roadblocks on the main routes into town, stopping the scooter and motor cycle riders and checking their driving documents. This gave the police a lot of information as to who they were and where they lived. A number were booked for traffic offences. The idea was to give them as much harassment as possible in the hope that it might turn some of them away. The police knew that they would be outnumbered during the weekend and had arranged for officers to be drafted in from neighbouring forces.

The rumours were right, as more and more scooter riders came into town and made their way to Madeira Drive and Kings Road. They rode up and down the seafront in convoys. These were soon stopped, as police stepped into the road and halted traffic, directing the scooters to the side of the road and letting other vehicles pass by. The scooter riders were then split into small groups, some being sent back the way they had come while their friends were sent in the opposite direction – another means of harassment.

As Friday evening came to a close most of the Mods had settled at the eastern end of Madeira Drive, their scooters lined up near the gardens at Black Rock. They were noisy, having their radios blaring, but this was by far the best place to have them. The police could keep an eye on them here. What the police didn't want was dozens

of Mods in the town centre. By around 1am many of them had settled down to sleep on the grassy bank at Black Rock, the noise
subsiding. This was the signal for the police to act, and three van-
loads moved in among the sleeping youths, waking them up. They
were questioned and their details checked. 'Why are you in
Brighton?' was an often-asked question. After about an hour the
police moved off and the Mods settled down once again. The idea
was to deny them sleep so that they might want to catch up on
during the day and not cause too much trouble in the town. Well,
that was the theory.

Sometime between 3am and 4am the police were back on the
scene, waking up the sleeping hordes and questioning them again as
to their names, addresses and the purpose of their visit to Brighton.
For many of them this was just about the last straw, and a number
got on their scooters and left the area. Most were never able to get
back to sleep and so sat on the grass lighting up their cigarettes until
the new day dawned. The police night shift had done a good job.

Their replacements (far more than usual) knew they were starting
a very long shift. They were divided into various groups, with a large
number being kept at the police station in reserve. The returning
vehicles were quickly cleaned and re-fuelled ready for the long day
ahead.

In the town centre patrols reported the gradual build-up of both
Mods and Rockers. Many officers were placed on static duty at the
railway station, as trippers and the youths poured into town and
headed straight down Queens Road and West Street towards the
seafront area. They were tracked by police motor cyclists, and any
group on scooters were stopped and asked for the production of
driving documents as well as their scooters being examined for any
traffic violations. It was essential that they were harassed as much as
possible and that the police were in command at all times.

The general idea was to herd the Mods onto the beach and keep
them there for as long as possible, the reasoning being that they
couldn't then run through the town smashing windows or causing
any other type of damage.

Every so often a group of Mods would suddenly run across the
beach for no apparent reason, while on other occasions they ran

towards some poor Rocker they had just spotted. This was a source of some amusement. The unfortunate individual running for his life wouldn't make the mistake of venturing down onto the beach again.

As the day wore on, more and more Mods and Rockers arrived in town, many closely shadowed by groups of police. A command centre had been set up so that the senior officers knew exactly what was happening at any given time: groups of officers radioed in from various parts of the town.

Brighton continued to fill with the youths. It also began to fill with sightseers, who lined all of the vantage points in order to get the best view of the proceedings. They wanted to watch the predicted fights and arrests that would surely follow. The officers who had been kept in reserve now found themselves being loaded into the blue water-works vehicles, eight or ten to a vehicle, depending on size.

The first major incident occurred about mid-morning when a group of some 50 Mods chased and cornered two Rockers. The two had tried to out-run the Mods but were caught. They were badly beaten, and after being rescued by police they were taken to the Royal

A bit of a knees up. Elderly visitors look on as Mods and Rockers clash by a shelter on the seafront. [Author's collection]

Sussex County Hospital, which had brought in more staff to cope with the expected extra patients. Six Mods were arrested at this incident and loaded into the waterworks vehicles.

At the police station some ten officers would take over from those involved in the arrests, searching the prisoners and placing them in the cells. This enabled the arresting officers to get back to the seafront area where they were most wanted. Gradually more fights broke out and officers rushed to quell them. A couple of groups managed to leave the beach and make their way into the Lanes area, where a number of shop windows were smashed. They also called into a cafe and assaulted two youths who they believed were Rockers. In fact they were just a couple of local lads, who refused hospital treatment and made their way home.

One fight occurred on the sun terrace of the Aquarium when a large crowd of Mods armed themselves with deck chairs and attempted to crown a small group of Rockers. The Rockers, unable to escape, jumped from the terrace to the pavement below and ran off at a rare pace. A large number of police had made their way to the scene and they were just arriving when the Rockers jumped over the balustrade. We had managed to witness part of this fight, and so five more Mods were arrested. Many of them were very young, averaging 15 or 16 years.

As there were many officers on duty we were able to return to the police station for a half-hour break during the day. Quite a number of these Rockers were happy, when in a group, to give the police a fair amount of cheek. They soon realised, however, that the police were in no mood to accept this.

Time and time again information reached us that another group of Mods had been arrested for a variety of offences. This continued throughout the day – and this was only Sunday, with the bank holiday still to come.

It had been arranged between the police and the courts that the magistrates would sit each day to hear the evidence and mete out suitable punishment to the wrong doers. As evening came the cells were bulging: more than 75 people had been arrested on this one day. A number of them were juveniles, which meant that their parents or guardians would need to attend the police station. Many of the youngsters didn't realise this would happen and were terrified of the consequences. The older ones appeared at the magistrates court and if they pleaded not guilty, as many did, they were remanded in custody for a week and taken to Lewes Prison.

For many officers this had been a very long and tiring day. A 12-hour shift had been the minimum, while others involved with prisoners would do more. But just about every officer on duty thought it had been a very good day: interesting, to say the least. For many it had been like the old days, with the implementation of the Ways and Means Act and officers clipping a few ears of those hell bent on causing trouble. Oh yes, for the police a very satisfying day.

Sunday night followed the same pattern as the previous night, when officers keeping the Mods from a decent night's sleep. It seemed to work, for there had been many seeking sleep on the beach during the day. It rained on and off for most of the night. This deterred them from wandering about and made sure that they would stay at the far end of Madeira Drive.

Monday duly arrived. The early shift reported for duty and more and more officers joined them. Officers from the surrounding forces would join us as the day progressed: they, too, wanted some of the action.

There were several 'runs' across the beaches. This had the public getting quite excited as to what was going to happen next, but more often than not the Mods suddenly stopped and sat down on the shingle. On one occasion a small group of five police officers, including a sergeant, saw a group of about two hundred Mods running towards a slope that would bring them up to the promenade. The police quickly formed a line across the top to block their path, me among them. The teenagers continued to run up the slope, and when they were close to the top the sergeant ordered us to draw our truncheons. The Mods displayed a very threatening attitude, but although we knew we were probably going to get hurt, we were determined to defend ourselves. As it happened our fierce attitude was enough to turn the large group away, and they quickly returned to the beach.

Throughout the morning many scuffles occurred between the Mods and Rockers ,and also among the various groups of Mods. More arrests followed. The police had organised 'snatch-squads' who would go onto the beach and arrest one of the ring-leaders.

With large numbers of officers on duty the weary early-turn officers were allowed to take regular breaks. They were still very tired, and this resulted in an occasional show of frustration. Some arrested Mods were handled roughly, especially when they put up a struggle. The police were determined to teach them a lesson and to put them off ever returning to Brighton for their fights.

A number of ring-leaders who had been watched for most of the day were rounded up and put into a large waterworks van. The policemen who were using this vehicle made their young charges comfortable in the back of the van, removing their shoes, shoelaces and trouser belts. They were then run out of town – driven up towards the Devils Dyke and deposited at the junction with the Saddlescombe Road. The youths, mostly from the London area, stood demurely in a group, wondering what was going to happen. Nothing! The policemen watched as they slowly made their way along the road en route to their London homes.

About 50 yards away from where the officers were, they stopped and started to thumb a lift. The officers took up a position on the road leading to the main London Road and stopped the vehicles that came along, advising drivers not to pick up any hitchhikers that they might see thumbing a lift to London. Some twenty minutes later, with the group out of sight, the policemen returned to their van and headed back to the seafront.

Meanwhile the numbers of arrests continued to grow, the magistrates sitting for most of the day. At about 5pm the youths who had come by train started to make their way towards the railway station accompanied by large numbers of policemen who would ensure that they would cause no damage to the shops as they passed. Many were herded into the station, surrounded by the police. By this time it was generally accepted that the Mods had had just about enough of Brighton, some admitting that it had been a horrible weekend and that the police had been very brutal. The police agreed with this, making it quite clear to them that should they ever return it would be a lot worse.

As they arrived at the station they were directed to two platforms

Both of them had trains heading for Victoria, and the youths were given no option but to board them, even if they lived in Brighton. Each train held a sufficient number of Policemen as travelling companions.

At Victoria they were greeted by a large contingent of Metropolitan officers, together with dogs and horses. By this time all the fight had gone out of the youths, and all they wanted to do was to get home.

As the last of them left town, there was a sigh of relief. It had been a very busy but, for most of the policemen on duty, an unusual and interesting experience. A sight that many officers will never forget was the help offered and given by a number of well known barrow boys and petty criminals who were so incensed that these people had the audacity to invade our town that they joined in and on several occasions meted out summary justice upon the heads of both the Mods and Rockers. One barrow-boy, for instance, gave a youth a 'leather injection' (a hefty kick in the rear) when to his mind he didn't move quickly enough after being directed to move on by a police officer. The police officer simply turned his head and failed to witness the incident.

A week later, the Mods and Rockers who had been on remand in Lewes Prison attended the magistrates court. The chairman of the bench, Mr. Cushnie, had previously indicated that anyone who appeared before him would be severely dealt with. As the youths appeared in court, one by one, those present couldn't help but let out a gasp: these youths were almost unrecognisable from those that had been arrested a week before. Their looks had certainly changed as on arrival in prison it had been advisable, for health reasons, to shave their hair. Standing in the dock, they were close to being bald.

For those convicted of breach of the peace and other similar offences, heavy fines were imposed. Those convicted of any type of damage were heavily fined and had to pay a large slice of the costs of the damage. For anyone convicted of assault, it was in the main a prison sentence. Addressing many of those facing him in the dock, Mr Cushnie said, 'I will not have you people coming here to destroy our town and upset both the residents and the visitors whom we hold most dear.' He was passionate about his town of Brighton.

There was one very sad event during the course of that bank holiday weekend. A small group of youths had camped out on the cliff top at Saltdean. When they woke next morning one of them was missing. His body was later found at the foot of the cliffs.

The Mods and Rockers phenomenon carried on for several years, although not on quite such a large scale. All bank holiday police leave was cancelled for years, because it was imperative that the force had available as many officers as was possible. And just as Brighton police had called in assistance from other parts of the county, so there was a time when officers from Brighton repaid the compliment at Hastings.

In the main the youths certainly deserved to be arrested and receive their just punishment. However, looking back over the forty years that have now passed, I wonder just what actually happened as regards two of the most common offences – 'obstructing the police' (seven youths were arrested for this) and, more seriously 'assaulting a policeman'.

I mention these two offences although I have no particular knowledge about those arrested for them on this day. I would simply like to point out that it did seem at times that the same police officers were repeatedly assaulted or obstructed. Let me make it quite clear that I am not saying that in these cases there was anything untoward, but during almost 27 years of police service in Brighton I was assaulted only three times and obstructed only once. These were genuine offences and those arrested were punished.

Some *Evening Argus* reports in the days after the troubles:

It was reported that police were engaged in traffic checks on the A23 at the Pylons. Just before noon on Whit Monday a coach full of teenagers was stopped and ordered to return to London. Brighton Police had been tipped off by the Metropolitan Police. The driver had little option but turn his coach around and head northwards.

It was reported that 27 youths, mostly from the London area appeared before a Special Court on Bank Holiday, Monday 18th May 1964, during the afternoon. At least another 20 were expected to appear before Magistrates in the evening.

The charges included five of possessing offensive weapons, two of stealing milk, seven for obstructing police, one for assaulting a policeman, one of throwing stones, eleven for using threatening or insulting behaviour, one for wilful damage to a deckchair and three for discharging missiles.

Robert Peel, 19 years, of Broderick House, Kingswood Estate, West Dulwich SE 2; was jailed for three months and fined £2 at Brighton magistrates court on Monday 25th May 1964 for using insulting behaviour and discharging a missile – namely a deckchair on the Aquarium Sun Terrace during the Whit Monday disturbances.

James Shiels, 19 years, of Grenville Place, Brighton pleaded 'not guilty' to discharging a missile -- namely a deckchair. Police Constable Peter Gregory said, 'A fight, involving a large number of girls and youths suddenly broke out [on the Aquarium Sun Terrace] and deckchairs were thrown.' He went on, 'I saw Shiels take up a deckchair and throw it over the balcony to the pavement below.'

Giving evidence, Shiels said, 'I and three friends were surrounded by 200 Mods, who were shouting, "Rockers!" They started throwing stones and I picked up a deckchair to protect my face.'

Shiels' friend, Tony Fowler of Ryde Road, Brighton, who was called as a witness said, 'We were surrounded. There was nothing we could do. We didn't throw deckchairs. It wasn't worth it against a crowd like that.'

The magistrates found Shiels guilty and he was fined £2 for the offence.

Christopher John Withers, 17 years, of Portland Road, Hove, pleaded 'not guilty' to using insulting behaviour during the Whitsun disturbances and having an offensive weapon -- a belt.

It was alleged that he told police, 'If I got into a fight with the Mods and Rockers, I would have used it, wouldn't you?'

Police Constable Basil Baverstock said in court, 'I saw Withers, who was dressed as a Rocker, among a group in West Street, Brighton. They were jostling pedestrians and forcing them to walk around the group. I saw Withers put his hand inside his jacket and thought he had an offensive weapon.'

The magistrates found Withers guilty and he was fined £20.

BEATLEMANIA

It may seem strange for me to be writing about the two most famous pop groups of the 1960s – the Rolling Stones and the Beatles – but I came into contact with both groups as a policeman in 1964.

I was on a week's late shift in October of that year. The Beatles were due to play two concerts at the Hippodrome in Middle Street and great crowds were expected. They had started their tour of Britain on the 9th October in Bradford. We had been told a couple of weeks prior to their concert that many of us would be working in the town centre on 'A' Division on the date of the concert. All police leave days were cancelled for the event, as it was pretty obvious that we would all be needed, mainly for crowd control. The young people of the town were all very excited and proudly boasted at having a ticket for the concerts.

As it happened I was a great Beatle fan myself, and I looked forward to the chance of seeing and hearing these four young guys who were world famous. It seemed that every record that they released was a massive hit and immediately shot to the top of the hit parade. I was hoping I would be able to get a duty within the Hippodrome building so that I could see and hear them.

They were going to play two evening concerts on Sunday 25th October, the first one starting at 6pm. I was on duty in Middle Street at around 2pm, and although we shut the road it was thronging with excited and very vocal young people. As the afternoon passed the crowds grew considerably, all eager to get a look at the Beatles. The details of their schedule had been kept secret and was known only to the senior officers who were there in numbers.

The man in charge of the operation was Superintendent Alan Probyn, and he had obviously used a considerable amount of local knowledge in planning the Beatles' arrival and exit. He had also arranged for around forty policemen to be in attendance both inside and outside the Hippodrome.

With a view to giving any first aid treatment, a 20-strong group of

St. John Ambulance people were also in attendance, under their superintendent, Ted Sanderson. They took over Middle Street Primary School as a first aid post and were to treat 18 young girls, most of them suffering from emotion and hysteria.

Almost opposite the Hippodrome theatre was the GPO garage (now BT.). This garage stretched from West Street to Middle Street with entrances in both streets. At the appointed time, and on a signal from one of the senior officers, the doors of the garage in Middle Street opened and four lads dressed in washed denims raced across Middle Street and into the Hippodrome. This happened so quickly that I am sure that the crowds didn't realise that the Beatles had arrived.

Once they were safely in the theatre, several of us were moved to different locations. I got my dream job. I was to work in the Hippodrome's auditorium immediately in front of the stage to stop the young fans jumping onto the stage. First, though, I had yet another job – and that was to be on John Lennon's dressing room door. At least that was the job I was told to do, but what followed made that impossible.

The four Beatles had no intention of sitting alone in their rooms. They continually changed from one dressing room to another, full of fun, noisy and very excited. They took the mickey out of each other, as well as of the two of us who were there for security reasons. The fans were let into the theatre, and even at the back of it the noise could easily be heard.

It was soon time for the Beatles to go on stage, and at a signal I moved out into the theatre and the extremely noisy auditorium. I took my place in the front with about a dozen colleagues, looking out at a sea of faces, shouting out their favourite Beatle's name, each one trying to shout louder than their friends. The announcer then called out each name: 'George, Ringo, John and Paul, The Beatles!' Then with a great crescendo of noise, the curtains opened and there they were in their familiar suits and haircuts, their own distinctive look.

The screams from the young audience raised a number of decibels and was truly deafening. It was impossible to hear the Beatles playing their familiar hit songs. The temperature inside the theatre was stifling, and many young girls fainted and needed first

aid. Many of the young audience had become so excited that they had wet themselves. Although everyone had a seat, no one was sitting down: everyone was standing to get the best possible view.

While the band played their very famous and popular songs items continually flew from the audience onto the stage. There was the usual hail of jelly babies, thrown with some accuracy by the screaming girls. These were followed by a huge number of dolls, then programmes, toilet rolls and screwed up paper, on which were scribbled messages addressed to the group.

We knew that at some point the girls would charge down the aisles and try to get onto the stage. We were ready, and when it happened it was easy to stop them. They were told to return to their seats, but none did, probably because they couldn't hear what we were saying, added to the fact that they didn't want to.

There was a short intermission and then they were back, singing in full voice while the young girls continued to shout and scream. The concert eventually came to an end and we returned to the dressing room area. They were pouring sweat, having worked very hard to entertain their young fans, but they were very happy and taking their fill of liquid refreshment and food. The theatre was cleared and after some clearing up and cleaning it was soon time to let in the second house. By this time I was finding it very difficult to hear: I had been totally deafened by the noise and there was a time when I wondered if my hearing would return as normal. I had wanted to see the Beatles, and had been given a wonderful opportunity to do just that, but now I wasn't quite sure that I wanted to go through it all again. There was no chance of changing my job, however. I had been detailed for that specific task and in those days nothing was changed.

It was soon time for the second show to start and I took my place once more in front of the stage. The second show was exactly the same as the first – the deafening noise, the excitement of the young people and the Beatles giving it all they had. At the end they came on for an encore and went off again. The audience were shouting their heads off for them to come on yet again but that wasn't to happen. While they were on stage, their belongings had been gathered up, and while the people waited they were whisked away, out of the building, across the road and back into the GPO garage. They got into the chauffeur-driven car, the garage doors opened and they were quickly on their way via West Street. The audience were still shouting for their heroes to come back, but the Beatles were by that time a long way away from the Hippodrome and heading north

The concert also included the American recording star Mary Wells, who had sung her heart out during the evening, but it was the Beatles that the young fans had come to see and hear.

Now, with everyone gone, there was only one noise that could be heard in the Hippodrome and that was the shuffling sound of the brooms sweeping up tons and tons of paper and other rubbish. After all, there was a variety show to get ready for Monday evening.

It took several days before my hearing returned to normal, and I was actually worried that it had received long-term damage. Deep down, however, I was as excited as some of those 4,000 young people who had made up the audience.

The deputy manager of the Hippodrome, Edward Evers, later said that he and his staff were forced to scour the theatre for around two hours making sure that none of the teenaged fans had hidden themselves inside. The staff even searched behind the stage and up on the roof, taking particular note of the tops of the adjacent buildings.

The *Evening Argus* carried a report of the concert in its Monday edition, and one reader took exception to it. Janet Dyball's letter appeared in the Thursday edition:

> *Contrary to your report . . . George did not look defiant and Ringo did not 'carry on regardless'. The Beatles looked very happy and smiled nearly all the time. Paul's charming smile never left his face.*
>
> *Furthermore, they did not sneak quietly away, as you stated. I saw them come out. They got into their car and Paul looked round and waved to me, still smiling, but looking rather tired. The Beatles were gear, but your reporter doesn't seem to like them.*

A few weeks later I again found myself on duty in Middle Street, this time for a Rolling Stones concert. I recall several differences between the two events. The crowd, though still young, were older by several years. The five members of the Stones arrived the same way, through the GPO garage, but they were dressed very smartly and, unlike the Beatles, changed to scruffy clothes to go on stage. Their concert was also very noisy, but this time I managed to get a position near to the back of the auditorium

This was my first brush with famous people and events, but it wouldn't be the last.

GOING TO THE DOGS

Before 1965 the Brighton Police Dog Section consisted of just two dogs and handlers, Pcs John Bray and Len Patterson. When a dog was retired in those days the handler had a choice – give up his dog (which might mean that it was put to sleep) and take on a new one or keep his dog and leave. When Len Patterson's dog was about to retire he decided to leave. Then there was a most sought after vacancy in the dog section and I thought I might fancy the job. By this time Pc Peter Gibson had joined the section, so that its staff numbered three.

The original Brighton Dog Section: Pcs John Bray (left) and Len Patterson. [Author's collection]

The dog section came under the Traffic Section, and I had an interview with Superintendent Field, who was in charge of it. I can recall telling him that my family had always had dogs and that I was very experienced. I can now come clean and admit that that wasn't quite true. The family had had a cocker spaniel for some years and I 'occasionally' took it out for a walk, which was just about the extent of my dog experience.

I must have impressed the superintendent nevertheless, as a few days later I was called to his office and given the job. However, there was a little 'kick-back' with the job. I was then living in Warren Way, Woodingdean, and I was told that the family would have to move from there into a 'dog house' at No. 1 Auckland Drive, Lower Bevendean. I wasn't very happy about this arrangement, but the family agreed that we should move, and the police did help with the moving expenses.

We packed our things and moved into Auckland Drive. There were two houses with a police box between them. The occupants of the other attached house were an experienced constable, Bob

Hampton, and his two children. The very sad thing was that Bob had just lost his wife, and the day we moved in was the day of her funeral. Bob was very kind – he was a jovial guy – and bearing in mind his circumstances he did what he could to help us settle down in our new surroundings. I have to say, though, that I never liked either the house or the area: it all seemed so alien to me.

Constable John Bray, who was in charge of the section, lived just down the road in Heath Hill Avenue, and it had been his suggestion that the Auckland Drive house be converted into a dog house, although all the kennels were portable. We got together to do some easy puppy training a few weeks later. I soon came to realise that it wouldn't be the dog that had to be trained but me.

We went down in a black Morris 8 van to a large kennels at Ticehurst to meet a breeder of alsatians, Mrs. Ann Butler, and find a puppy for me to train. I was very impressed with her. She stood no nonsense and had so many dogs about the place that it was impossible to count them all. In fact I'm not sure that she herself knew exactly, but it was more than 50 in all, including some delightful puppies. We were there some time and given lunch and a couple of pints of beer. They kept the beer in a barrel in one of the outhouses and it was almost a case of help yourself. I looked at the litter of puppies that were ready to take away and choose a lovely red sable dog with enormous feet. I knew this was going to be my dog as it kept licking me and just took to me as if we had known each other all our lives.

I believe the breeder asked around £15 for the eight-week-old puppy. She then offered another one, tan and gold in colour, saying that the force could have both for £20. John telephoned the chief constable, Bill Cavey, to tell him of the offer and asked what to do. He immediately told him to buy both, and said another dog handler would be appointed for the second puppy.

We put the two puppies into the van and set off back to Brighton. What we didn't know at this time was that they had been eating a concoction of horrible things, including manure and muck as well as their morning feed, all mixed with a quantity of milk. On the way back both puppies were sick, and the sway of the vehicle made matters worse as they lay in it and this soaked their coats. We stopped a few times and attempted to clean it up as best we could,